'THOU SHALT NOT STAND IDLY BY'

'Thou Shalt Not Stand Idly By'

Jews of Conscience on Palestine

Susan Landau

https://www.openbookpublishers.com

©2025 Susan Landau (Introductions and Notes)

This work is licensed under the Creative Commons Attribution-NonCommercial 4.0 International (CC BY-NC 4.0). This license allows you to share, copy, distribute and transmit the text; to adapt the text for non-commercial purposes of the text providing attribution is made to the authors (but not in any way that suggests that they endorse you or your use of the work). Attribution should include the following information:

Susan Landau, *'Thou Shalt Not Stand Idly By': Jews of Conscience on Palestine*. Cambridge, UK: Open Book Publishers, 2025, https://doi.org/10.11647/OBP.0481

Copyright and permissions for the reuse of some of the images included in this publication differ from the above. This information is provided in the captions and in the list of illustrations. Every effort has been made to identify and contact copyright holders and any omission or error will be corrected if notification is made to the publisher.

Further details about Creative Commons licenses are available at
https://creativecommons.org/licenses/by-nc/4.0/
All external links were active at the time of publication unless otherwise stated and have been archived via the Internet Archive Wayback Machine at https://archive.org/web

Digital material and resources associated with this volume are available at
https://doi.org/10.11647/OBP.0481/resources

Information about any revised edition of this work will be provided at
https://doi.org/10.11647/OBP.0481

ISBN Paperback: 978-1-80511-668-4
ISBN Hardback: 978-1-80511-669-1
ISBN PDF: 978-1-80511-670-7
ISBN HTML: 978-1-80511-672-1
ISBN EPUB: 978-1-80511-671-4
DOI: https://doi.org/10.11647/OBP.0481

Cover image: Olive tree in the Negev Desert in Israel. Photo by gkuna at iStock, under the iStock Content License, https://www.istockphoto.com/photo/olive-tree-in-desert-gm1257201732-368355323
Cover design: Jeevanjot Kaur Nagpal

Contents

Author's Bio	vii
About the Book	ix
About the Author	xiii
I. RECLAIMING JEWISH VOICES OF CONSCIENCE ON ISRAEL-PALESTINE	**1**
I.1 "A Land Without a People"	3
I.2 The Zionist Idea	7
I.3 Judaism Is not Zionism	13
I.4 On Occupation	17
I.5 On Divestment	21
I.6 On Peace and Justice	25
II. AMPLIFYING JEWISH VOICES OF JUSTICE ON ISRAEL-PALESTINE	**31**
II.1 Democracy, Equality, Refugees	33
II.2 Apartheid and Boycott, Divestment, and Sanctions (BDS)	37
II.3 Zionism, Then and Now	43
II.4 Nonviolent Activism	47
II.5 As a Jew	53
II.6 Antisemitism and Interfaith Relations	57

III. ENGAGING JEWISH VOICES OF CONSCIENCE AND DISSENT, POST 7 OCTOBER 2023   61

III.1 Initial Responses: In the Aftermath of 7 October 2023	65
III.2 Considering the Context: Settler Colonialism, Supremacy, and Hubris	71
III.3 Unbending the Arc: Genocide, Complicity, and Responsibility	77
III.4 Critical Distinctions: Antisemitism, Zionism,and Judaism	87
III.5 Praying With Our Feet: Jewish Values in Action	93
III.6 A Moral Reckoning:Statements of Conscience	99
III.7 The College Campus: Dissent, Repression, and Resistance	105
III.8 Affirming the Prophetic: Hope in Action	111
Acknowledgements	115
Voices	117
Notes	131

Author's Bio

Susan Landau is a passionate advocate for kindness, justice, truth, and equality. The time-honored ethical tradition of Judaism grounds her self-definition as an anti-Zionist Jew, and shapes over twenty years of her active engagement in learning, organizing, educating, writing, and advocating for justice for all people of historic Palestine. She offers presentations, classes, and webinars locally, and at regional and national conferences. Susan is a co-editor of a study guide, *Why Palestine Matters: The Struggle to End Colonialism* (2018, Palestine Justice Network of the Presbyterian Church, USA).

Susan Landau, LCSW is a Licensed Clinical Social Worker. She combines her lifelong career as a psychotherapist with a commitment to political education and advocacy in support of justice in Palestine. Susan lives in East Falls, Pennsylvania where she maintains her private psychotherapy practice.

About the Book

Overview

"Thou Shalt Not Stand Idly By" appears in the Old Testament, Book of Leviticus 19:16. This statement forms the bedrock of the moral imperative for justice. It affirms the responsibility of all beings for the welfare of each other and for the earth. The Hebrew prayer, the Shema: *"Hear, O Israel: The Lord our God is one"* (*Deuteronomy 6:4-9*) serves as the centerpiece of Jewish life. It asserts the preciousness of all life and the interconnectedness of all people. The ethical tradition of Judaism is embodied in these principles. There is a proud history of Jewish people who, in upholding these values, have spoken out in response to injustice, including injustice committed in the name of Jews.

For decades, prominent Jews have voiced dissent in response to the idea and realization of the Zionist project to establish and maintain a Jewish homeland in historic Palestine. A commitment to Judaism's ethical tradition of justice centers this dissent. Despite the need for Jewish safety in a post-Holocaust world and claims of entitlement to the biblical home of the Jewish people, moral objections have focused on how a Jewish state impacts the indigenous population living in Palestine.

Israel's destruction of Gaza since October 2023 is unparalleled in scale, even as it continues a decades-long policy. This moment screams dissonance between Zionism and Judaism, and must be addressed. *Thou Shalt Not Stand Idly By: Jews of Conscience on Palestine* does that in a uniquely accessible format. Building upon two previously self-published booklets, this book presents excerpts and quotations that readily lend themselves to further study, contemplation, critical thinking, and discussion. It advocates the reconsideration and relevance of this earlier wisdom in a post-7 October 2023 world and highlights an ongoing tradition of Jewish dissent to Zionism.

While other books may go into depth about specific individuals or focus on a particular time period, this volume includes the voices of more than 120 people over the course of decades, and even centuries. Some readers may prefer to read the book cover to cover and appreciate the magnitude and longevity of this dissent. Others may choose to flip through for specific topics or individuals, or use a quotation as a starting point for further exploration. This book lends itself to both approaches.

Structure

Part One: Reclaiming Jewish Voices of Conscience makes accessible, with poignant clarity and simplicity, the warnings and caveats of past and current Jewish thinkers, scholars, and activists as they engage, reflect, and address their serious misgivings about the Zionist project and, later, the State of Israel.

This first section is a compilation of quotations from recognized dissident moral voices within the global Jewish community that span the period from early Zionism of the late nineteenth century through the establishment of the State of Israel and the dispossession of the Palestinian people in 1948, and into the decades beyond.

Early voices include Ahad Ha'am (Asher Ginsberg), who promoted cultural Zionism, rooted in Jewish values of equality and respect for the indigenous Arab population. Philosopher Martin Buber opposed Israel as a nationalist project because the rights of the Palestinians were denied. Judah Magnes, an important Jewish Reform rabbi in the United States and Mandatory Palestine, proposed a binational state; he withheld support from Israel as a Jewish state on ethical grounds. German-born theoretical physicist Albert Einstein acknowledged Israel's critical role in providing a home for Jews in dire need, while he vehemently opposed the militarism and the anti-Arab animus required to advance the project of Jewish statehood in Palestine. After the Holocaust, German political thinker Hannah Arendt also advocated binationalism.

Part Two: Amplifying Jewish Voices of Justice on Israel-Palestine further emphasizes how early forewarnings have been borne out over decades. Facts were created on the ground that deepen an understanding of the Israeli occupation's violations of Palestinian human rights. A growing wave of Jewish dissent followed Operation Cast Lead, the First Gaza

War in 2008. Jews of conscience witnessed this injustice, and some participated in nonviolent movements to resist it, such as the global movement for Boycott, Divestment, and Sanctions (BDS) against Israel until it complied with international law.

Part Three: Engaging Jewish Voices of Conscience and Dissent follows the tsunami of political and human shock waves from the 7 October 23 Hamas attack on Israel. While many doubled down on the coupling of Judaism with Zionism and the conflation of anti-Zionism with antisemitism, Jewish voices featured in this section provide ground from which to contextualize, analyze, and respond to 7 October 2023. They posit that these attacks can be understood as an inevitable consequence of the events, actions, and history of record documented in the two previous sections of this book. They also demonstrate a willingness to put everything on the line for their commitment to the values of equality, justice, and freedom, risking academic, professional, social, and legal consequences.

The words of the scholars, historians, theologians, religious leaders, human rights advocates, and journalists who appear throughout this book are essential reading in this unprecedented political time.

Scope

The first two sections are replicated almost exactly from the original booklets, and their introductions reflect the periods in which they were written. *Part One* was published as a booklet just prior to Operation Cast Lead, Israel's 2008–2009 War on Gaza. *Part Two* was published just prior to Operation Protective Edge, Israel's 2014 War on Gaza. It covers material written between 2008–2013, and also includes a few quotations from previous years that connect thematically to this time. *Part Three* begins on 7 October 23 and concludes at the close of December 2024. The decade prior to *Part Three* is not covered.

Material featured in this book, particularly from the first two sections, includes some people who identified themselves as Zionists, both cultural Zionists and even political Zionists. Some served in the Israeli army or were active in a range of Zionist institutions. One may assume that many of the people included would disagree with each other, and that some who died years ago would likely have continued to evolve and change their views over time. Inclusion of an individual in this book does not imply support for their positions, even those perspectives expressed in the featured quotes. They are selected as examples of dissent from the mainstream political Zionist project. These excerpts illustrate the trajectory of this critical discourse over time.

While this book includes multiple perspectives, there are individuals, organizations, and topics that are not prominently featured or absent altogether. These include groups like The Bund (founded in 1897), The Workmen's Circle (founded in 1900 and now called The Workers Circle), The American Council for Judaism (founded in 1942), The Israeli Black Panthers (founded in 1971), Breira (1973–1977), The New Jewish Agenda (1980–1992), and others. Also not reflected upon in depth are Jewish responses to Palestinian resistance movements prior to the 2005 call for Boycott, Divestment, and Sanctions against Israel, specifically the Great Revolt (1936–1939), the First Intifada (1987–1993), the Second Intifada (2000–2005), and The Great March of Return (2018–2019). Finally, it should be noted that the collection of people featured in this book are much whiter than the Jewish world at large, including the world of Jews critical of Zionism. The author takes responsibility for these omissions of identity, perspective, topic, and institution, and encourages readers to seek additional information for a more comprehensive understanding.

The methodology for collection and inclusion of material in this book is this author's conscience, an idiosyncratic fidelity to truth-telling, and an intuition to experience, articulate, and transcend moral darkness. This book relies on a personal passion for justice, love for Jewish values, and respect for serious scholarship. The reader is invited to engage with this material by deconstructing common narratives, upending basic assumptions, abandoning previously held foregone conclusions, and investigating cognitive dissonance. A willingness to bear discomfort is implicit in opening to this complexity. Welcoming dissent enriches understanding, cultivates relationships, transforms contentious discussion into conversation, and encourages collaboration toward the collective liberation of all people everywhere.

About the Author

I am an American woman, a Jew of conscience.

Liberation theologian Marc Ellis introduced the phrase 'Jews of Conscience' to designate Jews who have spoken out in a time he describes as the end of ethical Jewish history—the post-Holocaust era marked by Israeli statehood, the misuse of privilege and power, and the unremitting culpability of Jews in the occupation of Palestine. In his words, "There will always be Jews who speak truth to power. There will always be Jews who say no to injustice. There will always be Jews who refuse silence and accept exile rather than complicity in injustice."[1]

I love being Jewish, always have—family, community, holidays, stories, rituals, songs, prayers, and foods. That said, notwithstanding the encouragement of my parents, neither the state of Israel, nor Zionism, have ever been integral to or an expression of my Jewish identity.

My parents were ardent Zionists, passionate about their trips to Israel in the 1950s. They returned home with photos of camels, pictures of Hadassah Hospital, and a beautiful Yemenite bracelet that I grew to love. The Holocaust was never discussed, though family members died in the camps. As a teenager, I declined the popular summer kibbutz experience in Israel, preferring the diversity of my small-town friendships. I donated my extra pennies to UNICEF rather than putting them in the blue boxes at Sunday school where they would go to plant trees in Israel to "make the desert bloom."

The Israeli flag in the synagogue of my childhood occupied no space in my brain. I was proudly Jewish, absent the suggested *Ahavat Yisrael*—a loving connection to Israel. In fact, Israel did not much matter to me at all. This bears over-stating because one day, twenty-something years ago, everything changed.

I have thought about Israel and Palestine every day since then.

That day, my then 13-year-old son began a conversation with me about Israel. He had questions. To prepare, I brought home all the books about Israel from the congregational school library of the local progressive synagogue where we were members. As a teacher in the Sunday school, I had easy access. I carefully spread the books over the living room floor. I selected one, then another, showing my son the pictures and reading aloud basic facts about the state and the people. After listening for a while, Ben cautiously interrupted, "There's more to the story, mom." He recommended I read the two books he was holding, *The Fateful Triangle* by Noam Chomsky and *The Question of Palestine* by Edward Said. Surprised and concerned, I agreed. That day changed my life.

In addition to the books Ben gave me, I began to read the work of the Israeli "new historians"—Ilan Pappe, Benny Morris, Simha Flapan, and Avi Shlaim. Their research was based on newly disclosed Israeli documents revealing Israel's historical record from 1948, when Israel became a Jewish state. My initial shock came with the realization that Israel Independence Day was for Palestinians the Nakba, the Catastrophe, marking the dispossession and transfer of 750,000 indigenous Palestinians from their homes, and the destruction of their fields and property.

What consumed my attention about Israel, that day and since, were the injustices and human rights violations by Israeli Jews toward Palestinians. These facts seemed inconceivable, utterly un-Jewish. I had been taught to "Remember we were slaves in Egypt," to treat other people the way I would want to be treated.

Distraught and untethered, I reached out to a few people from our progressive Jewish community whom I remember commenting about Palestine; I had not understood, maybe even dismissed, what had been said. My friend Rachael Kamel was one of these people. Then employed at the American Friends Service Committee, Rachael invited me and my son to meet a Palestinian man, Jamal Juma. Jamal was touring the US, educating Americans about a huge illegal concrete barrier that Israel was building through Palestinian orchards and villages to confiscate land for the Israeli state. He showed us maps and books, explaining that Israel had recently begun building a wall both along the Green Line and inside the West Bank to separate Jewish Israelis from Palestinians, and Palestinian people from their land.

Appalled and eager to act, we participated in planning and attending a "Stop the Wall" demonstration at a downtown park in Center City Philadelphia. It was held on a Saturday. As Shabbat services concluded in nearby synagogues, some of their members surrounded our protest in a counter-protest. They sang Hebrew songs with vitriol, seemingly at us. My head was spinning. I was bewildered, yet in my gut I understood that I was being targeted as an antisemite.

That a Jewish state violated the core values of Jewish ethical tradition was anathema. Did others know about this? As a Jewish educator, I channeled my cycles of horror, shame, outrage, and betrayal into teaching what I was learning. I developed curricula for elementary and middle school classes at my congregation. The centerpiece of my teaching was simple and straightforward: being Jewish is a way of life evidenced by the choices we make every day about how to treat people in our families, our friends, neighbors, pets, and the environment.

For the older students, I prepared lessons that introduced the experience of Palestinians through comparisons with the Native American population in the US. As a class project, we collected and sent money to plant trees in Palestine. I engaged all levels of my congregation to learn the actual historical record of Israel's founding as a Jewish homeland, and to share the history and human stories of the Palestinian people. I offered an adult education class entitled "1948 through Film." We screened archival footage of Palestinian families in their pre-1948 villages. They lived in large, majestic homes they had built, cultivated orchards, planted and reaped fruits and olives on land that had been in their families for decades. The visuals were stunning, magnificent, and indisputable.

Despite my enthusiasm and stride, support from colleagues and parents of the children in my classes was not forthcoming. Quite the opposite—students whispered as I entered the classroom. The Education Committee challenged me. My reputation as a beloved teacher began to suffer. My synagogue was progressive except Palestine, a phenomenon so widespread it garnered its own acronym (PEP). I was stonewalled, then confronted. The accusation was that I had an antipathy toward Israel. Maybe I did. I knew that I no longer felt at home in my progressive Jewish synagogue community. I left.

I began speaking out as a Jew of conscience, though at the time I was unfamiliar with that phrase as a description of what was bubbling up inside me. I came to trust my commitment to truth-telling and my passion for justice; together they have been a reliable catalyst for my activism then and since. Every week I joined a vigil in front of the Israeli Consulate. We were a like-minded interfaith group. We held political signs and distributed informational literature educating about Israeli violations of Palestinian human rights. We marked Israel Independence Day by handing out pamphlets about the Nakba and released dozens of black balloons on the Philadelphia Parkway as the decorative blue and white floats celebrating Israel passed in their annual procession.

Eventually, grief over the loss of my congregational affiliation and beloved Jewish community faded, ushering in an exciting period of re-evaluation and reflection. Over time, through collaboration and solidarity, my dissent served to create and shape community. I discovered my place in solidarity as a Jew in the global movement for justice in Palestine, a Palestinian-led movement.

Through organizing intersectionally, more broadly, and in an interfaith context, I met allies with whom I shared universal values of justice, equality, and freedom. Drawing upon the bold history of the church standing up to injustice during the US Civil Rights Movement and the anti-Apartheid struggle in South Africa, Christians learning about Israeli violations of Palestinian human rights became natural allies. My role was to offer support in the face of actual or perceived claims of antisemitism. It was and continues to be important for Christians to engage in conversations with Jews in which their criticism of Israel is accepted and openly discussed.

As my network continued to expand, I met and made common cause with other anti-Zionist Jews. Together we developed creative liturgy, actions, and events to fuse our activism and values into shared Jewish rituals and holiday celebrations. I realized that my Palestine solidarity work had become the strongest expression of what being Jewish means to me.

A few years into this work, I co-edited a study guide, *Why Palestine Matters: The Struggle to End Colonialism* (2018). As a member of an interfaith teaching team, I participated in teaching a course based on the book, mostly in local faith-based communities. In a stunning acknowledgement of the shifts happening within the Jewish community, the synagogue I had left several years earlier warmly welcomed me to teach a course. Conversations on topics previously taboo were now on the table. We discussed the Nakba, apartheid, the right of return, and the 2005 call for Boycott, Divestment, and Sanctions (BDS) against Israel. I felt at home in my own skin and in the community. Several years later, as I was leaving a local Palestinian film screening, a member of that congregation caught my eye and approached me. She firmly took my hand, and spoke softly, "This is what you had been trying to tell us."

Marc Ellis (of blessed memory) dared to break with themes of Jewish power and nationality, instead insisting the prophetic voice in Judaism be reclaimed. I met Marc in 2008; we connected again before his death in 2023. Both encounters were poignant, brief, and, for me, life-altering. His books—underlined in colors and with my musings scribbled in the margins —are everywhere in my home. I spend time with them regularly, as I would a wise old friend. His brave exploration, soulful reflection, and prolific writing uncomplicate and refocus me in ways that every day resonate, revitalize, and reconfigure my practice of Judaism.

Whatever happens going forward will happen. It is important that the truth of what has happened and what is happening to Gaza, to the United States, and to the world, is recorded in a very deliberate way that will be accessible over time. This is my contribution to that record of truth.

I. RECLAIMING JEWISH VOICES OF CONSCIENCE ON ISRAEL-PALESTINE

Introduction

The height of nineteenth century European nationalism and colonialism marked a sharp rise in violence and repression against Jews. Imperiled, European Jews began to envision a Jewish homeland in historic Palestine. In 1897, the Zionist movement—committed to the proposition that Jews could be safe only in a country of their own—was launched by a small number of secular Jews. Caveats came from leaders within Zionist movement, such as Ahad Ha'am, Martin Buber, Judah Magnes, and others who promoted the establishment of a Jewish cultural or spiritual center within the region called Palestine, but not at the expense of the indigenous Palestinian population.

The Nazi Holocaust changed the terms of the debate and as such galvanized unflinching world support for political Zionism—a branch of the movement dedicated to the creation of a Jewish nation-state in Palestine. By 1945 most Eastern European Jewish communities were all but wiped out; most European Jews who had managed to survive the atrocities of World War II had no place to go. The United States in particular, but other Western powers as well, neither provided a place of refuge for surviving Jews, nor played a responsible role in facilitating a return to their countries of origin. Instead, the response to Jewish displacement and suffering was the partition of the British Mandate territory of Palestine by the United Nations in November 1947. The State of Israel was established on May 14, 1948.

Having a place to go where Jews would be safe and free from discrimination did not necessarily require exclusive Jewish sovereignty over the homeland of Palestinian Christians, Jews, and Muslims whose families had lived on this same land for centuries. However, this was the claim advanced by the Zionist leadership, and it gained momentum.

Jews of conscience began to speak out.

Having declared itself an independent nation-state, Israel was steadfast in its determination to create and maintain a demographic majority of Jews on the land. The Israeli government instituted expansionist policies to destroy Palestinian villages, expel or "transfer" the Palestinian population, and to occupy or repopulate areas so Palestinians could not return to their homes.

Jews of conscience continued to speak out.

Israel's victory in the 1967 "Six-Day War" concluded with its occupation of Palestinian territories including East Jerusalem, the West Bank ("Judea" and "Samaria"), and the Gaza Strip, as well as the Syrian Golan Heights and the Sinai Peninsula (returned to Egypt in 1978). The Geneva Conventions prohibit occupying countries from taking any actions to dispossess civilians living under occupation, or from making a state of occupation permanent. For the past forty years, Israel has done both.

Recognizing silence as complicity, Jews of conscience have spoken out.

Today Palestinians in the West Bank, Gaza, and East Jerusalem still live under Israeli military occupation, in violation of international humanitarian law and recognized principles of human rights. Israel continues to expand illegal Jewish settlements in the occupied territories, confiscate land and resources, demolish Palestinian homes and fields, build an apartheid wall through Palestinian communities, and implement against Palestinians brutal policies of detention, curfew, checkpoints, roadblocks and economic embargo.

In response to these policies, a growing number of American Jews actively challenge the unconditional support of the US government for Israeli policies that perpetuate the occupation and contribute to the senseless suffering of the Palestinian people. This includes opposing direct US military aid to Israel. These policies, and the foreseeable consequences of the Israeli occupation of the West Bank, Gaza, and East Jerusalem, are not sustainable. Jewish ethical tradition finds these actions, taken in our names, morally indefensible. Furthermore, they prejudice the well-being and ultimately imperil the survival of Jews and Judaism, both in Israel and throughout the world. Where we go from here depends on the resolve of ordinary people to tell the truth and to insist on justice.

As Jews of conscience, we will continue to speak out. Hear our voices!

Susan Landau, Spring 2008

I.1 "A Land Without a People"

The truth hurts like a thorn at first; but in the end it blossoms like a rose.
Shmuel Ha-Nagid, Ben Mishle

One thing we certainly should have learned from our past and present history and that is not to create anger among the local population against us. [...] We have to treat the local population with love and respect, justly and rightly. And what do our brethren in the Land of Israel do? Exactly the opposite! Slaves they were in their country of exile, and suddenly they find themselves in a boundless and anarchic freedom, as is always the case with a slave that has become king, and they behave towards the Arabs with hostility and cruelty, infringe upon their boundaries, hit them shamefully without reason, and even brag about it.[2]

Ahad Ha'am, 1891

I do not think that Palestine could ever become a Jewish state, nor that the Christian and Islamic worlds would ever be prepared to have their holy places under Jewish care. It would have seemed more sensible to me to establish a Jewish homeland on a less historically burdened land. But I know that such a rational viewpoint would never have gained the enthusiasm of the masses and the financial support of the wealthy.[3]

Sigmund Freud, 1930

For me, the Arab-Jewish struggle is a tragedy. The essence of the tragedy is a struggle of right against right. Its catharsis is the cleansing pity of seeing how good men do evil despite themselves out of unavoidable circumstance and irresistible compulsion. When evil men do evil, their deeds belong to the realm of pathology. But when good men do evil, we confront the essence of human tragedy. In a tragic struggle, the victors become the guilty and must make amends to the defeated. For me the Arab problem is also the Number One Jewish problem. How we act toward the Arabs will determine what kind of people we become: either oppressors and racists in our turn like those from whom we have suffered, or a nobler race able to transcend the tribal xenophobias that afflict mankind.[4]

I. F. Stone, 1969

I believe in a Zionism that faces facts, that exercises strength with restraint, that sees the Jewish past as a lesson, but neither as a mystical imperative or a malignant dream; that sees the Palestinian Arab as a Palestinian Arab [...]; a Zionism that is capable of seeing itself as others may see it; and finally, a Zionism that accepts the spiritual implications and the political consequences of the fact that this small but precious land is, *bon gré, mal gré*, the homeland of two peoples fated to live facing each other because no God nor angel will descend to judge between right and right. The lives of both depend on the hard, tortuous and essential process of learning to know each other in the strife-torn landscape of this beloved country.[5]

Amos Oz, 1978

Like most Israelis, I have always been under the influence of certain myths that had become accepted as historical truth. And since myths are central to the creation of structures of thinking and propaganda, these myths had been of paramount importance in shaping Israeli policy for more than three and a half decades. Israel's myths are located at the core of the nation's self-perception. Even though Israel has the most sophisticated army in the region and possesses an advanced atomic capability, it continues to regard itself in terms of the Holocaust, as the victim of an unconquerable, bloodthirsty enemy. Thus whatever Israelis do, whatever means we employ to guard our gains or to increase them, we justify as last-ditch self-defense. We can, therefore, do no wrong. The myths of Israel forged during the formation of the state have hardened into this impenetrable, and dangerous, ideological shield. Yet what emerged from my reading was that while it was precisely during the period from 1948 and 1952 that most of these myths gained credence, the documents at hand not only failed to substantiate them, they openly contradicted them.[6]

Simha Flapan, 1987

A central slogan of the Zionist movement declared that the Land of Israel is 'a land without people for a people with a land.' If Palestinians appear at all, it is as mere background, an undifferentiated mass of 'Arabs,' romantic peasants at best, at worst intractable enemies whose only role is to kill innocent Jews. The narrative reveals the very core of the Israeli-Palestinian conflict, which is not a denial of Jewish ties to the country *per se* but of Jewish claims that are exclusive, that do not make room for the other people living there. In what can only be described as a kind of autistic nationalism, the Zionist movement saw a lot of 'Arabs' living in the country but not a people with a distinctive national identity, legitimate claims to the land and a collective right of self-determination. The Arab presence was reduced to a non-issue or, as it was called in a 1906 Zionist tract, the 'Hidden Question.' [...] Unlike Western democracies whose civil societies are based on citizenship and are thus capable of incorporating people of different ethnic and religious backgrounds, Zionism adopted the tribal form of nationalism that privileges the group which 'owns' the country at the expense of 'intruders,' the Palestinians. [...] Since their own national claims have been deemed invalid, the Palestinians' presence is based on sufferance, not on right. This is true within Israel, defined as a 'Jewish democracy,' where 'Israeli Arabs' are required to recognize Israel as a Jewish state before they are allowed to run in elections. As far as the Occupied Territories are concerned, Israel reserves for itself the right to rule over the Occupied Territories, notwithstanding international law prohibiting it from taking any unilateral steps that render its occupation permanent. It has made it clear that only if the Palestinians accept Israel's 'generous offer' of a mini-state will the conflict end.[7]

Jeff Halper, 2005

I.2 The Zionist Idea

In ruling in a dispute between two people who claimed ownership of a tract of land, Rabbi Ezekiel Landau is reputed to have put his ear to the ground and then to have announced, 'The earth has rendered its decision: "I belong to neither of you, but both of you belong to me."

Rabbi Ezekiel of Prague (1713–1793)

I wish to place on record my view that the policy of His Majesty's Government is anti-Semitic and in result will prove a rallying ground for Anti-Semites in every country in the world.

This view is prompted by the receipt yesterday of a correspondence between Lord Rothschild and Mr. Balfour.

Lord Rothschild's letter is dated the 18th July and Mr. Balfour's answer is to be dated August 1917. I fear that my protest comes too late, and it may well be that the Government were practically committed when Lord Rothschild wrote and before I became a member of the Government. [...] But I do feel that as the one Jewish Minister in the Government I may be allowed by my colleagues an opportunity of expressing views.

[...]

[I]t seems to be inconceivable that Zionism should be officially recognised by the British Government, and that Mr. Balfour should be authorized to say that Palestine was to be reconstituted as the "national home of the Jewish people". I do not know what this involves, but I assume that it means that [Muslims] and Christians are to make way for the Jews and that the Jews should be put in all positions of preference and should be peculiarly associated with Palestine in the same way that England is with the English or France with the French.

[...]

I assert that there is not a Jewish nation. [...] It is no more true to say that a Jewish Englishman and a Jewish Moor are of the same nation than it is to say that a Christian Englishman and a Christian Frenchman are of the same nation.

[...]

When the Jews are told that Palestine is their national home, every country will immediately desire to get rid of its Jewish citizens, and you will find a population in Palestine driving out its present inhabitants.

[...]

I would say to Lord Rothschild that the Government will be prepared to do everything in their power to obtain for Jews in Palestine complete liberty of settlement and life on an equality with the inhabitants of that country who profess other religious beliefs. I would ask that the Government should go no further.[8]

Edwin Samuel Montagu, 1917

Our national desire to renew the life of the people of Israel in their ancient homeland, however, is not aimed against any other people. As they enter the sphere of world history once more, and become once more the standard bearer of their own fate, the Jewish people, who have constituted a persecuted minority in all countries of the world for two thousand years, reject with abhorrence the methods of nationalistic domination, under which they themselves have suffered. We do not aspire to return to the land of Israel with which we have inseparable historical and spiritual ties in order to suppress another people or to dominate them. In this land, whose population is both sparse and scattered, there is room both for us and for its present inhabitants.

Our return to the Land of Israel [...] will not be achieved at the expense of other people's rights.[9]

Martin Buber, 1921

If we cannot find ways of peace and understanding, if the only way of establishing the Jewish National Home is upon the bayonets of some European empire, our whole enterprise is not worthwhile.[10]

Judah Magnes, 1929

Judaism owes a great debt of gratitude to Zionism. The Zionist movement has revived among Jews the sense of community. [...] This productive work in Palestine [...] has saved a large number of our brethren from the direst need. [...]

Now the fateful disease of our time—exaggerated nationalism, born up by blind hatred—has brought our work in Palestine to a most difficult stage. [...]

I should much rather see reasonable agreement with the Arabs on the basis of living together in peace than the creation of a Jewish state. Apart from practical consideration, my awareness of the essential nature of Judaism resists the idea of a Jewish state with borders, an army, and a measure of temporal power no matter how modest. I am afraid of the inner damage Judaism will sustain—especially from the development of a narrow nationalism within our own ranks, against which we have already had to fight strongly even without a Jewish state.[11]

Albert Einstein, 1938

The slogan Jewish state or commonwealth is equivalent, in effect, to a declaration of war by the Jews on the Arabs.[12]

Judah Magnes, 1942

I oppose Zionism because I deny that Jews are a nation. We were a nation for perhaps 200 years in a history of four thousand years. [...] Certainly, since the Dispersion, we have not been a nation. We have belonged to every nation in the world. We have mixed our blood with all peoples. Jewish nationalism is a fabrication woven from the thinnest kinds of threads and strengthened only in those eras of human history in which reaction has been dominant and anti-Semitism in full cry.[13]

Rabbi Elmer Berger, 1943

Independence of one's own must not be gained at the expense of another's independence. Jewish settlement must oust no Arab peasant, Jewish immigration must not cause the political status of the present inhabitants to deteriorate, and must continue to ameliorate their economic condition. The tradition of justice is directed towards the future of the country as a whole as well as towards the future of the Jewish people. [...] A regenerated Jewish people in Palestine has not only to aim at living peacefully together with the Arab people, but also at a comprehensive cooperation with it in opening and developing the country. Such cooperation is an indispensable condition for the lasting success of the great work of the redemption of the land.

The basis of such cooperation offers ample space for including the fundamental rights of the Jewish people to acquire soil and to immigrate without any violation of the fundamental rights of the Arab people. As to the demand for autonomy, it does not, as the greater part of the Jewish people thinks today, necessarily lead to the demand for a 'Jewish State' or for a 'Jewish majority.' [...] I think that state and majority are not the necessary bases for Zionism.[14]

Martin Buber, 1946

The real goal of the Jews in Palestine is the building up of a Jewish homeland. This goal must never be sacrificed to the pseudo-sovereignty of a Jewish state. The independence of Palestine can be achieved only on a solid basis of Jewish-Arab cooperation. [...] Elimination of all [Jewish] terrorist groups [...] will be the only valid proof that the Jewish people in Palestine has recovered its political reality and that Zionist leadership is again responsible enough to be trusted with the destinies of the Yeshuv.[15]

Hannah Arendt, 1948

To underscore the obvious: the Zionist Movement, from the start, could not help but injure and impinge on the rights of the people who lived in the country. Furthermore, the belief that a Jewish state with non-Jewish citizens can be a democracy guaranteeing equal rights to all is not tenable, and the practice of a quarter-century simply demonstrates that what was to be expected did in fact occur.[16]

Noam Chomsky, 1975

A defining moment in my life and journey as a child of Holocaust survivors occurred even before I was born. It involved decisions taken by my mother and her sister, two very remarkable women, which would change their lives and mine. After the war ended, my Aunt Frania desperately wanted to go to Palestine to join their sister, who had been there for ten years. The creation of a Jewish state was imminent, and Frania felt it was the only safe place for Jews after the Holocaust. My mother disagreed and adamantly refused to go. She told me many times during my life that her decision not to live in Israel was based on a belief, learned and reinforced by her experiences during the war, that tolerance, compassion, and justice cannot be practiced or extended when one lives only among one's own. 'I could not live as a Jew among Jews alone.' She said, 'For me, it wasn't possible and it wasn't what I wanted. I wanted to live as a Jew in a pluralistic society, where my group remained important to me but where others were important to me, too.'

Frania immigrated to Israel and my parents went to America. It was extremely painful for my mother to leave her sister, but she felt she had no alternative. (They have remained very close and have seen each other often, both in this country and in Israel.) I have always found my mother's choice and the context from which it emanated remarkable.[17]

Sara Roy, 2002

In a world where nations and peoples increasingly intermingle and intermarry at will; where cultural and national impediments to communication have all but collapsed; where more and more of us have multiple elective identities and would feel falsely constrained if we had to answer to just one of them; in such a world Israel is truly an anachronism. And not just an anachronism, but a dysfunctional one.[18]

Tony Judt, 2003

I.3 Judaism Is not Zionism

If I am not for myself, who will be for me? If I am for myself alone, then what am I? And if not now, when?

Rabbi Hillel, Pirkei Avot 1:14

Apart from the political danger, I can't put up with the idea that our brethren are morally capable of behaving in such a way to humans of another people, and unwittingly the thought comes to my mind: if it is so now, what will be our relations with others if in truth we shall achieve at the end of times power in Eretz Israel? And if this be the 'Messiah': I do not wish to see his coming.[19]

Ahad Ha'am, 1912

We will have to understand that Jewish suffering during the Holocaust no longer will serve as protection, and we certainly must refrain from using the argument of the Holocaust to justify whatever we do. To use the Holocaust as an excuse for the bombing of Lebanon, for instance, as Menachem Begin does, is a kind of 'Hilul Hashem' [sacrilege], a banalization of the sacred tragedy of the Shoah [Holocaust], which must not be misused to justify politically doubtful and morally indefensible policies.[20]

Nahum Goldman, 1981

Jews are defined by neither doctrine nor credo. We are defined by task. That task is to redeem the world through justice. [...] The War on Lebanon has now made clear to me that the resumption of political power by the Jewish people after two thousand years in the Diaspora has been a tragedy of historical dimensions. The State of Israel has demanded recognition as the modern political incarnation of the Jewish people. To grant that is to betray the Jewish tradition. [...]

I now conclude and avow that the price of a Jewish state is, to me, Jewishly unacceptable and that the existence of this (or any similar) Jewish ethnic-religious nation state is a Jewish, i.e. a human and moral, disaster and violates every remaining value for which Judaism and Jews might exist in history. The lethal military triumphalism and corrosive racism that inheres in the State and its supporters (both here and there) are profoundly abhorrent to me. So is the message that now goes forth to the nations of the world that the Jewish people claims the right to impose a holocaust on others in order to preserve its State.[21]

Henry Schwarzschild, 1982

I have concluded that one way to pay tribute to those we loved who struggled, resisted, and died is to hold on to their vision and their fierce outrage at the destruction of the ordinary life of their people. It is this outrage we need to keep alive in our daily life and apply it to all situations, whether they involve Jews or non-Jews. It is this outrage we must use to fuel our actions and vision whenever we see any signs of the disruptions of common life: the hysteria of a mother grieving for the teenager who has been shot; a family stunned in front of a vandalized or demolished home; a family separated, displaced; arbitrary and unjust laws that demand the closing or opening of shops and schools; humiliation of a people whose culture is alien and deemed inferior; a people left homeless without citizenship; a people living under a military rule. Because of our experience, we recognize these evils as obstacles to peace. At those moments of recognition, we remember the past, feel the outrage that inspired the Jews of the Warsaw Ghetto and allow it to guide us in present struggles.[22]

Irena Klepfisz, 1988

Jewish communities in the so-called Diaspora need to live in their here and now, 'constructing a harmony' within the world. This implies the reverse of the ethos 'solidarity with Israel.' Instead of lumping everything together, it is time to make distinctions—between Judaism and Zionism, Israeli and Jew, the biblical and the political. When everything is lumped together, judgment goes to pieces. Why else do so many Jews of goodwill and sound mind persist in defending the indefensible when it comes to Israel? Making distinctions allows those who care about the state to offer something better than blind, unconditional support: cool, careful, measured, qualified, sustained, candid criticism—the kind you cannot give unless you are at one removed. This is solidarity worth its salt. At the same time, it means making room within Jewry for all Jews, including those who feel no tie to Israel.[23]

Brian Klug, 2002

The failure of Israel to be a liberal democracy and a nation-state of the Jews is well known, and I hope I don't have to bring the familiar arguments. That fact that Israel is a settler-state founded on the thwarted national dreams of a native population compounds the problem, but, frankly, there would be problems even if Israel had been founded in a wilderness bereft of people.

But while Israel has, I believe, failed as a liberal state of the Jews, it need not be a failure as a liberal nation-state of all its people of the Israeli people, Jews and non-Jews, Palestinians and Jews. [...]

For Zionism to flourish in a liberal democracy, one cannot have a Jewish state as constituted now. The law of return would have to be abolished—in its stead could be an immigration law which favors certain groups (Jewish and Palestinian) but does not grant citizenship automatically to any quasi-religio-ethnic group. In such a state, one would not be forever counting heads to see whether there is a Jewish majority—because at every moment, the state would consist of 100% of Israeli citizens.

People say to me, 'Why would any Jew be interested to live in a state like that?' The funny thing is that the Jews who ask me this question actually do live in a state like that—it is called the USA.

Other people say, 'Hang on, but what happens in your Israeli state if a majority of its citizens are able to change the constitution in such a way as to reduce the Jewish component to a minimum?' My answer is simple: in that case, the citizens would have every right to do so. But so what? What's the point of a predominant culture if most of the state's citizens are opposed to it. That is like saying that the idea of America is a bad one, because in principle, most of the citizens could change the constitution and vote America out of existence. Yes, but so what?[24]

Jerry Haber, 2007

I.4 On Occupation

Not only one who cuts down trees, but also one who smashes household goods, tears clothes, demolishes a building, stops up a spring, or destroys articles of food with destructive intent transgresses the command, 'You must not destroy.'

Maimonides, Mishneh Torah, Laws of Kings and Wars 6:8, 10

A peace which comes from fear and not from the heart is the opposite of peace.

Gersonides

Israeli policy in the occupied territories is one of self-destruction of the Jewish state, and of relations with the Arabs based on perpetual terror. There is no way out of this situation except withdrawal from the territories.[25]

Yeshayahu Leibowitz, 1976

The frightening metamorphosis that is coming over us [...] places in question the justice of the Zionist movement; the basis for the existence of the state, but it receives no attention in the Knesset, the World Congress, the World Zionist Organization (then in session in Jerusalem), or elsewhere. It is time to recognize there is no such thing as an enlightened occupation; there cannot be a liberal military administration.[26]

Yoram Peri, 1982

Israel's occupation of Palestine is the crux of the problem between the two peoples and it will remain so until it ends. For the last 35 years, occupation has meant dislocation and dispersion; the separation of families; the denial of human, civil, legal, political and economic rights imposed by a system of military rule; the torture of thousands; the confiscation of tens of thousands of acres of land and the uprooting of tens of thousands of trees; the destruction of more than 7,000 Palestinian homes; the building of illegal Israeli settlements on Palestinian lands and the doubling of the settler population over the last ten years; first the undermining of the Palestinian economy and now its destruction; closure, curfew, geographic fragmentation, demographic isolation and collective punishment.

The Israeli occupation of the Palestinians is not the moral equivalent of the Nazi genocide of the Jews. But it does not have to be. No, this is not genocide but it is repression, and it is brutal. And it has become frighteningly natural. Occupation is about the domination and dispossession of one people by another. It is about the destruction of their property and the destruction of their soul. Occupation aims, at its core, to deny Palestinians their humanity by denying them the right to determine their existence, to live normal lives in their own homes. Occupation is humiliation. It is despair and desperation. And just as there is no moral equivalence or symmetry between the Holocaust and the occupation, so there is no moral equivalence or symmetry between the occupier and the occupied, no matter how much we as Jews regard ourselves as victims.[27]

Sara Roy, 2002

The Zionist revolution has always rested on two pillars: a just path and an ethical leadership. Neither of these is operative any longer. The Israeli nation today rests on a scaffolding of corruption, and on foundations of oppression and injustice. As such, the end of the Zionist enterprise is already on our doorstep. There is a real chance that ours will be the last Zionist generation. There may yet be a Jewish state here, but it will be a different sort, strange and ugly.

There is time to change course, but not much. What is needed is a new vision of a just society and the political will to implement it. Nor is this merely an internal affair. Diaspora Jews for whom Israel is a central pillar of their identity must pay heed and speak out. If the pillar collapses, the upper floors will come crashing down. [...]

It turns out that the 2,000-year struggle for Jewish survival comes down to a state of settlements, run by an amoral clique of corrupt lawmakers who are deaf both to their citizens and to their enemies. A state lacking in justice cannot survive.[28]

Avraham Burg, 2003

Through the checkpoints, road closures, movement ban, and traffic restrictions, through the concrete walls and barbed wire fences, through the land expropriations (solely for the purpose of security, as the High Court of Justice, which is part and parcel of the Israeli people, likes to believe), through the disconnecting of villages from their lands and from a connecting road, through the construction of a wall in a residential neighborhood and in the backyards of homes, and through the transformation of the West Bank into a cluster of 'territorial cells,' in the military jargon, between the expanding settlements Israelis have created and continue to create an economic, social, emotional, employment and environmental crisis on the scale of a never-ending tsunami.

In other words, we push an entire people into impossible situations, blatantly inhumane situations, in order to steal its land and time and future and freedom of choice, and then the plantation owner appears and relaxes the iron fist a bit, and is proud of his sense of compassion. [...]

And among all the details, the reality of colonialism intensifies, without letup or remission, inventing yet more methods of torture of the individual and community; creating more ways to violate international law, robbing land behind the legal camouflage, and encouraging collaboration out of agreement, neglect or torpor.[29]

Amira Hass, 2005

We have always said: the occupation corrupts. Now it has to be said with a clear voice: the occupation is endangering the security of Israel.[30]

Uri Avnery, 2006

Peace will not be achieved without the inclusion of the Gaza Strip in political agreements, and without the complete removal of settlements in the Occupied Territories and the termination of all forms of occupation, siege, and economic oppression. Only peoples with the ability to realize basic human rights, who have freedom of movement, who are able to develop and live at ease, can guarantee peace treaties. No agreement that is based on starvation and oppression can endure. Prevention of fuel and basic necessities, with severe repercussions on the lives of over a million inhabitants, will not end missile attacks. On the contrary it will provoke a bloody war of attrition.[31]

Joel Beinin, 2007

At the end of the day, it is the facts on the ground that speak most clearly. One can only wonder what Israeli Prime Minister Olmert is thinking when he talks about a viable Palestinian state while actively making such a dream unreachable.

Perhaps a more honest name for the current madness is not the realization of the Road Map, but rather the steady creation of Road Blocks that are rapidly crushing the hopes of the majority of Israelis and Palestinians for a viable two-state solution.[32]

Alice Rothchild, 2007

I.5 On Divestment

And they shall beat their swords into plowshares, and their spears into pruning hooks; Nation shall not lift up sword against nation, neither shall they learn war anymore.

Isaiah 2:4

The hysteria over a new anti-Semitism hasn't anything to do with fighting bigotry—and everything to do with stifling criticism of Israel.[33]

Norman Finkelstein, 2005

We are asking the city of Somerville, as well as other cities and civic institutions, to divest from companies involved in selling arms, bulldozers and military technologies that are used by the Israeli army to commit war crimes against Palestinians.

As people committed to human rights for all, we call upon Americans to demand that their tax-dollars are not invested in companies that sell equipment and ammunition that fuel Israel's consistent and appalling violations of international law and human rights.

As a young soldier serving in the Israeli army, I was ordered to commit war crimes in the Palestinian Occupied Territories. My platoon meted out collective punishment on whole Palestinian communities, shot live ammunition at unarmed civilians, killed women and children, enforced prolonged curfews, creating humanitarian disasters, arrested and detained Palestinians without charge, demolished their homes, and arbitrarily destroyed crops and property.

Being an eyewitness to these war crimes led me eventually to announce my refusal to serve in the Occupied Palestinian Territories in 1994. But the Israeli government, unaffected by the growing 'refusenik' movement, has continued the dehumanizing Occupation.

More than 3.5 million Palestinians continued to live under a military regime and were subject to bombings of neighborhoods, extra-judicial killings, torture, home demolitions, unlawful detentions, deportations and a myriad of human rights violations.

[...]

I have heard too many times the argument that *'now is not the time to divest because Israel is involved in a peace process.'* The 'peace process' argument was used for dozens of years as an excuse to continue inflicting suffering, humiliation and destruction upon the Palestinians in the West Bank and Gaza.

It is high time to do away with this myth. It has become clear that even during the Oslo process, Israeli governments pulled the wool over the world's eyes. Israel continued to resettle its own citizens on confiscated Palestinian land in the Occupied Territories, in violation of Article 49 of the Fourth Geneva Convention, while at the same time entrenching a cruel military regime in the same areas and punishing 3.5 million Palestinians.

It became the primary objective of Israeli propaganda to hide the brutal reality of Occupation. To this end, Israeli governments constantly came up with 'peace plans' and built a sophisticated 'we only want peace' propaganda machine.

Over time, many of us who lived in Israel and visited or served in the Occupied Territories, saw the reality for what it is: Israel was intensifying an oppressive military regime over millions of Palestinians who were denied all human, civil and political rights, while building more Jewish-only settlements for Jews who enjoyed full civil and political rights.

As an Israeli thoroughly familiar with Israeli politics, I believe that selective economic pressure is the most effective way to end the brutal Occupation of the West Bank and Gaza, and bring peace and security to Israelis and Palestinians.

I realize how hard it is, conceptually, for American Jews to support divestment, but they should understand that these painful measures will eventually lead to the path of peace and security. The call for divestment reflects true loyalty both to Israel's peaceful existence and to the highest Jewish values.

I call upon the Jewish community, as well as other communities, in the US—if you really want to see in your lifetime Israelis living in peace with Palestinians—unite with us behind divestment resolutions.[34]

Shamai Leibowitz, 2005

I.5 On Divestment

The story of the Gaza evacuation shows that international pressure can lead Israel to concessions. The reason the U.S. exerted pressure on Israel, for the first time in recent history, was because at that moment in time it was no longer possible to ignore the world discontent over its policy of blind support of Israel—the U.S. had to yield to international public opinion. This also shows the limits of power and propaganda. Despite the silencing of criticism of Israeli policies in Western political discourse, the fight for justice for the Palestinian people has penetrated global consciousness. The fight has in spread in the West by persistent individuals—a few courageous journalists who insist on covering the truth, despite the pressure of an acquiescent media and pro-Israel lobbies, solidarity movements that send their people to the occupied territories and take part in vigils at home, professors who sign boycott and divestment petitions, subjecting themselves to daily harassment. Often this fight for justice seems futile; nevertheless, it has had an effect on public opinion, which in turn can force governments to act.[35]

Tanya Reinhart, 2006

On this stage, not so long ago, I claimed that Israel is conducting genocidal policies in the Gaza Strip. I hesitated a lot before using this very charged term and yet decided to adopt it. [...]

On 28 December 2006, the Israeli human rights organization B'Tselem published its annual report about the Israeli atrocities in the occupied territories. Israeli forces killed this last year six hundred and sixty citizens. The number of Palestinians killed by Israel last year tripled in comparison to the previous year (around two hundred). According to B'Tselem, the Israelis killed one hundred and forty-one children in the last year. Most of the dead are from the Gaza Strip, where the Israeli forces demolished almost 300 houses and slew entire families. This means that since 2000, Israeli forces killed almost four thousand Palestinians, half of them children; more than twenty thousand were wounded.

B'Tselem is a conservative organization, and the numbers may be higher. But the point is not just about the escalating intentional killing, it is about the trend and the strategy.

And one should never tire of stating the inevitable political conclusions from this dismal reality of the year we left behind and in the face of the one that awaits us. There is still no way of stopping Israel than boycott, divestment and sanctions. We should all support it clearly, openly, unconditionally, regardless of what the gurus of our world tell us about the efficiency or *raison d'etre* of such actions. The only soft point of this killing machine is its oxygen lines to 'western' civilization and public opinion. It is still possible to puncture them and make it at least more difficult for the Israelis to implement their future strategy of eliminating the Palestinian people by ethnically cleansing them in the West Bank or the Gaza Strip.[36]

Ilan Pappé, 2007

A true friend of Israel, one that is sincerely concerned for its fate, is only that friend who dares to express sharp criticism of its policy of occupation, which poses the most serious risk to its future, and who also takes practical steps to end it. Most of the 'friendly' statesmen do not understand this. [...]

Blind friendship enables Israel to do whatever it wants. The days have passed in which every mobile home erected in the territories and every targeted assassination were carefully considered out of fear of international criticism. That time no longer exists. Israel has a carte blanche to kill, destroy and settle. The U.S. long ago gave up the role of honest broker.[37]

Gideon Levy, 2008

I.6 On Peace and Justice

'Justice, justice, you shall pursue.' This means: pursue justice justly. The verse teaches us that the methods we use to pursue justice must be just.

Rabbi Simcha Bunim of Peshischa, Itturei Torah

Palestine does not belong to the Jews and it does not belong to the Arabs, nor to Judaism or Christianity or Islam. It belongs to all of them together; it is the Holy Land. If the Arabs want an Arab national state in Palestine, it is as much or as little to be defended as if the Jews want a national state there. We must once and for all give up the idea of 'Jewish Palestine' in the sense that a Jewish Palestine is to exclude and do away with an Arab Palestine. This is the historic fact, and Palestine is nothing if it is not history. If a Jewish national home in Palestine is compatible with an Arab national home there, well and good, but if it is not, the name makes little difference. The fact is that nothing there is possible unless Jews and Arabs work together in peace for the benefit of their common Holy Land. It must be our endeavor first to convince ourselves and then to convince others that Jews and Arabs, Moslems, Christians, and Jews have each as much right there, no more and no less, than the other: equal rights and equal privileges and equal duties. That is practically quite sufficient for all purposes of the Jewish religion, and it is the sole ethical basis for our claims there. Judaism did not begin with Zionism, and if Zionism is ethically not in accord with Judaism, so much the worse for Zionism.[38]

Judah Magnes, 1929

One who, like myself, has cherished for many years the conviction that the humanity of the future must be built up on an intimate community of nations, and that aggressive nationalism must be conquered, can see a future for Palestine only on the basis of peaceful cooperation between the two peoples who are at home in the country. [...] I believe that the two great Semitic peoples, each of whom has in its way contributed something of lasting value to the civilization of the West, may have a great future in common, and that instead of facing each other with barren enmity and mutual distrust, they should support each other's national and cultural endeavors, and should seek the possibility of sympathetic cooperation. I think that those who are not actively engaged in politics should above all contribute to the creation of this atmosphere of confidence.[39]

Albert Einstein, 1930

Israel should choose the way of 'active neutralism,' by calling on all nations of the world, East and West, to join in exploring ways and means for the solution of a problem endangering the peace of the Middle East and the world, which can only be solved when *all* peoples of the region and all the great powers combine in a constructive effort: the problem of the Arab refugees.

We propose that the Israeli Government should make a solemn declaration that it is prepared to allow the return to its territory of Arab refugees—without fixing any definite figure—and to pay compensations under the condition that all interested parties (the Arab states, the refugees, the U.N. and the great powers) will cooperate with Israel in the discussion and execution of plans for the resettlement of the refugees in Israel and the Arab states.[40]

Martin Buber, 1957

One lesson [learned from the Nazi holocaust] is that being reduced to ashes does not ennoble a people. Another is that placing others into the ashes does not heal us of the previous trauma. Instead it increases the trauma by emptying us of the very resources that allowed us to survive with our dignity intact in the first place. It may be that survival without dignity is survival without meaning. [...]

Surely Jews and Palestinians are learning the limitations of nationalism, that pretenses to innocence are illusions and that dreams of empowerment often become nightmares in reality. [...]

There will always be Jews who speak truth to power. There will always be Jews who say no to injustice. There will always be Jews who refuse silence and accept exile rather than complicity in injustice. There will always be Jews who speak and live the prophetic in the ashes and beyond. The commanding voices of Sinai and Auschwitz demand no less of us. They can be heard only in the calls to end the cycle of violence and hatred that has engulfed the Jewish people and that now ties us irrevocably to the Palestinian people.

And herein lies the hope for the future. Jews of conscience in concert with others can continue to chart an alternative way of life even in exile. For Jews and Palestinians in Israel/Palestine can begin to act as if the divisions between Israel and Palestine do not exist and as if solidarity with one another is the norm.[41]

Marc Ellis, 2002

Israel, in an amazingly short time, has degenerated into heartlessness, real cruelty towards the weak, the poor, and the suffering. Israel displays indifference to the hungry, the elderly, the sick and the handicapped, equanimity in the face of, for example, trafficking in women, or the exploitation of foreign workers in conditions of slave labor; and in the face of profound, institutionalized racism toward its Arab minority. When all this happens as if it were perfectly natural, without outrage and without protest, I begin to fear that even if peace comes tomorrow, even if we eventually return to some sort of normality, it may be too late to heal us completely.

The calamity that my family and I suffered, when my son Uri fell in the war last summer, does not give me any special privileges in our national debate. But it seems to me that facing death and loss brings with it a kind of sobriety and clarity, at least when it comes to distinguishing the wheat from the chaff, between what can and cannot be achieved. Between reality and fantasy.

[...]

Appeal to the Palestinians, Mr. Olmert. [...] Appeal to the Palestinian people. Speak to their deepest wound, acknowledge their unending suffering. [...] Hearts will open a bit to each other, and that opening has great power. Simple human compassion has the power of a force of nature, precisely in a situation of stagnation and hostility.

Look at them, just once, not through a rifle's sights and not through a roadblock. You will see a people no less tortured than we are. A conquered, persecuted, hopeless people. [...] But look at them for a moment in a different way. Not just at their extremists. Not just at those who have an alliance of mutual interest with our own extremists. Look at the great majority of this wretched nation, whose fate is bound up with ours, like it or not.

Go to the Palestinians, Mr. Olmert. Don't look for reasons not to talk to them. You've given up on unilateral disengagement. And that's good. But don't leave a vacuum. [...] Go to them with the boldest, most serious plan that Israel is able to put forward, a plan that all Israelis and Palestinians with eyes in their heads will know is the limit of refusal and concession, ours and theirs. [...]

Perhaps, Mr. Prime Minister, I need to remind you, that if any Arab leader sends out signals of peace, even the slightest, most hesitant ones, you must respond. You must immediately test his sincerity and seriousness. You have no moral right not to respond. You must do so for the sake of those who will be expected to sacrifice their lives if another war breaks out.[42]

David Grossman, 2006

I am an Israeli patriot, and I do not feel that I need anybody's recognition of the right of my state to exist. If somebody is ready to make peace with me, within borders and on conditions agreed upon in negotiations, that is quite enough for me. I am prepared to leave the history, ideology, and theology of the matter to theologians, ideologues, and historians.[43]

Uri Avnery, 2007

Justice requires first that Israel acknowledge the truth of its responsibility for dispossession and for denying the refugees their right to return. There must be an effort to recognize the legitimacy of international law, to restore lost lands and human rights, including the right of self-determination. The search for justice for Palestinians, so long denied their human and national rights, continues. The goals of ending occupation and establishing equal rights for all, based on international law and human rights, remain absolute.[44]

Phyllis Bennis, 2007

I.6 On Peace and Justice 29

Remains of the village of Zarnuqa depopulated during the 1948 Nakba. Over two thousand Palestinian residents were forcibly displaced from approximately 7,545 dunams of their land by Zionist forces in May 1948 during "Operation Lightening."
Photo by: Omri Eran Vardi. Activestills Photo Collective, all rights reserved.

II. AMPLIFYING JEWISH VOICES OF JUSTICE ON ISRAEL-PALESTINE

Introduction

Six years have passed since the 2008 printing of *Thou Shalt Not Stand Idly By: Reclaiming Jewish Voices of Conscience on Israel-Palestine*. Its ongoing appeal, to Jews and non-Jews alike, is a tribute to the prescient voices of those who, prior to 1948, warned of the ethical consequences of establishing a Jewish state in historic Palestine, as well as those who in later years have made an unambiguous case against the unjust Israeli occupation and ongoing Nakba in Israel-Palestine.

In 2008, Israel drastically tightened its regime of sanctions on Gaza. The Israeli invasion of Gaza in December of that year was an atrocity on a grand scale, obliterating Gaza's infrastructure, demolishing hospitals, schools, mosques, massacring the population, and making life unlivable. The aggressive and disproportionate use of force by the Israeli Defense Force was calibrated to ensure maximum suffering on the civilian population trapped in Gaza. The international community was stunned, its conscience stirred.

In the aftermath, the United Nations commissioned the Goldstone Report to investigate the Gaza action. Several international flotillas organized to shine light on the blockade and to bring humanitarian aid to break the siege of Gaza.

Despite irrefutable documentation of war crimes and the international outcry, these efforts were neutralized by the alliance and dominance of Israel and the United States.

Little has changed for the people in Gaza. Or in Palestine more broadly.

There is encouragement to be found in the fact that over time the parameters of the conversation have shifted, most noticeably in Europe, Australia, Canada and the United States. Since its launch by Palestinian civil society in 2005, the global movement for Boycott, Divestment, and

Sanctions until Israel complies with international law continues to gain traction and is building a steady track record of successes worldwide.

The global movement for justice and equality in Israel-Palestine is interfaith, intergenerational, and consistent with Palestinian demands for self-determination and equality. American Jews participate as activists and allies in solidarity with Palestinians, and as citizens whose government funds systemic injustice against Palestinians.

The land of historic Palestine is imbued with deep meaning for Christians, Muslims, and Jews. It has been the experience of this author that faith-based as well as secular communities offer distinct opportunities to educate and advance just action on local, national, and international levels.

The decision to limit the scope of these pamphlets to Jewish voices is intended to draw attention to the fact that as Jews, we are very much a part of this global movement. But to read this as a 'privileging' of the role of Jews in Palestine solidarity work would be inaccurate. Justice is a fundamental human issue and as such must be within the purview and mandate of all humanity.

Amplifying Jewish Voices *of* Justice *on* Israel-*Palestine* supplements the original pamphlet with a post-2008 selection of Jewish American and Israeli academics and activists who are unwavering in their commitment to justice for all peoples of the region.

Susan Landau, January 2014

II.1 Democracy, Equality, Refugees

What is hateful to you, do not to others. That is the entire law; all the rest is commentary.

Rabbi Hillel

For Israelis, to recognize the Palestinians as victims of Israeli actions is deeply distressing, in at least two ways. As this form of acknowledgement means facing up to the historical injustice in which Israel is incriminated through the ethnic cleansing of Palestine in 1948, it calls into question the very foundational myths of the State of Israel, and it raises a host of ethical questions that have inescapable implications for the future of the state.[45]

Ilan Pappé, 2008

The problematic definition of a Jew according to the Law of Return—'A Jew is a person who is born to a Jewish mother or who converted and is not of a different religion'—should be abolished, along with the old-fashioned concept of the nation-state. Israel should become the democratic state of the Jewish people which belongs to all of its citizens, and the majority will decide on its character and essence.[46]

Avraham Burg, 2008

Any sustainable peace is dependent upon the just resolution of the refugee issue. […] It depends on a package of three elements: Israel's acknowledgement of the refugees' Right of Return; Israel's acknowledgement of its responsibility in creating the refugees' plight;

and only then, technical solutions involving a mutually agreed-upon combination of repatriation, resettlement elsewhere, and compensation.[47]

Jeff Halper, 2008

My request is, therefore, that you persist and will not give up your right to return. Please, you and your children, don't ever give up your right to return. Not [only] for yourselves but for me also. Do you understand? If you give up this right all chance for a just life in this land will be lost and I will be sentenced to the shameful life of an eternal occupier, armed from the soles of my feet to the depths of my soul and always afraid, like all colonizers. […] Our humanity is bound up with your right to return. The day we expelled you from your land you carried a part of it with you. Only when you can return we will be able to restore our humanity.[48]

Eitan Bronstein, 2010

In 2005, with help from American marketing executives, the Israeli government began a marketing campaign, 'Brand Israel,' aimed at men ages 18 to 34. […] The government later expanded the marketing plan by harnessing the gay community to reposition its global image. […] The growing global gay movement against the Israeli occupation has named these tactics 'pinkwashing': a deliberate strategy to conceal the continuing violations of Palestinians' human rights behind an image of modernity signified by Israeli gay life.[49]

Sarah Schulman, 2011

No matter the potential merits and good will of the founding plan, the effort to establish and sustain the Jewish character of the intended Jewish democracy doomed the democratic character from the start, and it's been spiraling downward ever since. For whatever the starting point was, I think we mostly agree that Israel has become less democratic in recent years, and every time the separation between religion and state dwindles, free speech is curtailed, or minority rights are trampled, it is [...] in the name of preserving the state's Jewish character—that is, Jewish hegemony.⁵⁰

Marilyn Kleinberg Neimark, 2013

If Israel is to be considered a democracy, the non-Jewish population deserves equal rights under the law, as do the [Arab Jews] who represent over 30 percent of the population. Presently, there are at least twenty laws that privilege Jews over Arabs within the Israeli legal system. The 1950 Law of Return grants automatic citizenship rights to Jews from anywhere in the world upon request, while denying that same right to Palestinians who were forcibly dispossessed of their homes in 1948 or subsequently as the result of illegal settlements and redrawn borders.⁵¹

Judith Butler, 2013

In response to the United Nations' decision to recognize Palestine as an observer state, the Israeli government announced radical expansion of Jewish settlement in sensitive areas of Jerusalem and the West Bank. Jews living in Palestine thousands of years ago are cited to justify a right of 21st century Jews to 'return,' while Palestinian demands to return after 65 years of exile are deemed absurd.⁵²

Ian Lustick, 2013

How do we understand a Jewish 'right of return' to Israel that grants automatic citizenship to any Jew anywhere in the world while denying that same right to the very people who actually lived on this land not long ago? And can any 'return' truly be complete as long as it denies that right to others?⁵³

Rabbi Brant Rosen, 2013

The crisis of the imagination amongst Israeli citizens and Jews in the world is an added tragedy on top of occupation and apartheid. Zionists and their supporters are not able to conjure up an image of a society in which all citizens are equal and in which liberties and freedoms are shared. Israeli society can neither imagine that the return of Palestinian refugees can liberate them as well—liberation from the shackles of a Masada mentality, from white supremacy and from fear.[54]

Elisha Baskin, 2013

The international community should be getting the message loud and clear. Israel refuses to stop taking Palestinian land and expects to get what it wants in negotiations as well.[55]

Adam Horowitz, 2014

As Ariel Sharon proclaimed before the Knesset in 2002, Palestinian citizens of Israel (or those he called 'Israeli Arabs') had 'rights in the land,' but 'all rights over the Land of Israel are Jewish rights.' Each time an Arab party attempted to challenge the Jewish majority's unlimited control over state land policy and laws, they could expect to be met with sustained harassment, legal persecution, and official suppression. For Israel's Palestinians, challenging Jewish legal and political privilege was considered a form of high treason.[56]

Max Blumenthal, 2013

II.2 Apartheid and Boycott, Divestment, and Sanctions (BDS)

You shall have one law for stranger and citizen alike.
Leviticus 24:22

Last week, with initial hesitation but finally strong conviction, I endorsed the Call for a U.S. Cultural and Academic Boycott of Israel. [...] Until now, as a believer in boundary-crossings, I would not have endorsed a cultural and academic boycott. But Israel's continuing, annihilative assaults in Gaza and the one-sided rationalizations for them have driven me to re-examine my thoughts about cultural exchanges. Israel's blockading of information, compassionate aid, international witness and free cultural and scholarly expression has become extreme and morally stone-blind.[57]

Adrienne Rich, 2009

The question is not 'Is Israel the same as South Africa?'; it is 'Do Israel's actions meet the international definition of what apartheid is?' And if you look at those conditions which includes the transfer of people, multiple tiers of law, official state segregation, then you see that yes, it does meet that definition—which is different than saying it is South Africa. No two states are the same. It's not a question, it's a distraction. [...] The real reason, and what we really can learn from the South African example, is that when you have a relatively small trade-dependent state, this is a tactic that can actually work.[58]

Naomi Klein, 2009

But the greatest success of the BDS movement is its effect on the discourse. Here in the U.S., campaigns playing out in mainstream churches, shopping centers, university campuses, and city councils have fundamentally shifted the question from whether or not Israel is committing crimes to what are we going to do about it.[59]

Anna Baltzer, 2010

Consumed by hate, emboldened by self-righteousness, and confident that it could control or intimidate public opinion, Israel carried on in Gaza as if it could get away with mass murder in broad daylight. But while official Western support for Israel held firm [...] the Gaza invasion appeared to mark a turning point in public opinion reminiscent of the international reaction to the 1960 Sharpeville massacre in apartheid South Africa.[60]

Norman Finkelstein, 2010

Courageously and creatively, BDS faces violence with a firm commitment to nonviolence. It stands in solidarity first and foremost with Palestinians, and then with humanity—with the thousands of internationals and Israelis who have chosen nonviolent resistance as their means to oppose and end the oppression of Palestine. [...] BDS is a means to justice for those to whom it has been denied. Not against, but rather for, both Israel and Palestine, it aims to end the policies destroying the lives of Palestinians and devouring the humanity of Israelis. BDS supports the livable, viable futures of all the people of this land.[61]

Rela Mazali, 2010

Israel has many real security needs. But I have come to know that the ways in which the occupation of the West Bank is enforced go way beyond those needs to the realm of harsh discrimination and ready violence, aided by a complicit military and government.

This is all preface to my main point to you: I have changed my mind about the purchase of products made in the Jewish West Bank. All the rabbis I spoke to in Israel, who were not only RHR rabbis, are not buying West Bank products. I have decided to join them. Therefore, I will no longer oppose those who refuse to buy Ahava products.[62]

Rabbi Ellen Lippmann, 2011

The most accurate way to describe Israel today is as an apartheid state. [...] The only way to counter the apartheid trend in Israel is through massive international pressure. [...] Consequently, I have decided to support the BDS movement. [...] The objective is to insure that Israel meets its obligations under international law, and that Palestinians are granted the right to self-determination.[63]

Neve Gordon, 2012

Many people are offended by the description of Israel as an apartheid state. What we should be offended by is the actual policies that Israel employs against Palestinians. [...] Use of the term 'apartheid' applies whenever a state codifies into law a preferred identity status, then racializes that identity. The racialized identity group is systematically segregated from the rest of the population into discrete geographic areas (bantustans in South Africa; and areas A, B and C plus Gaza in Israel) in order to dominate and control them. An apartheid state grants the preferred group access to resources and benefits and denies the same benefits to the denigrated group. [...] Military repression, mass incarceration and unyielding bureaucracy are used to keep systems of apartheid in place.[64]

Rabbi Lynn Gottlieb, 2012

It may be that the movement of boycott, divestment, and sanctions is as much a struggle for healing as it is for justice. Could it be that justice is the only way to heal both martyred peoples, and that one's healing cannot take place without the healing of the other?[65]

Marc Ellis, 2012

Gaza is often described as the world's largest open-air prison. Israel maintains a draconian and brutal blockade of Gaza, and its Navy enforces this humanitarian catastrophe with HP information technology. Caterpillar has long sold specially designed bulldozers to Israel for its ongoing demolition of Palestinian homes. Motorola supplies Israel with surveillance equipment for use on illegal, Jewish-only settlements on Palestinian land.

These companies are actively enabling and benefiting from Israel's dispossession, control, and imprisonment of Palestinian civilians. [...] Divestment is a nonviolent action to urge these companies to quit selling technology and equipment that facilitate illegal policies and criminal actions against the Palestinian people. [...] Ending Israel's occupation is the only way to truly invest in Palestine.[66]

Hedy Epstein, 2012

Our immediate solution? Open up genuine discussions in the Jewish communities around the world about the occupation, the wall, and the right of return. Stop the tactics of calling one's opponents anti-Semitic or claiming that they advocate the 'elimination of Israel' when they are simply examining problems that must be addressed to eliminate injustice and uphold our tradition of 'Justice, justice thou shalt pursue.'

Long term, whether there is one state or two states or a federation of states or some kind of binational arrangement, what matters is that it must be a just solution based on equal rights and respect and safety for all. Until that happens, BDS is here to stay.[67]

Donna Nevel and Dorothy M. Zellner, 2012

Anyone who really fears for the future of the country needs to be in favor at this point of boycotting it economically. [...] The distinction between products from the occupation and Israeli products is an artificial creation. It's not the settlers who are the primary culprits but rather those who cultivate their existence. All of Israel is immersed in the settlement enterprise, so all of Israel must take responsibility for it and pay the price for it. There is no one unaffected by the Occupation, including those who fancy looking the other way and steering clear of it. We are all settlers [...] with Israel getting itself into another round of deep stalemate, both diplomatic and ideological, the call for a boycott is required as the last refuge of a patriot.[68]

Gideon Levy, July 2013

Israel is doing what a state committed to being a Jewish state has to do. It's taken over the entire territory and dealing with the inconvenient reality of non-Jewish inhabitants, and the inevitable outcome is what we have now, which is apartheid. Although the accepted story is that a two-state solution is on the table, what you have now effectively is one state, an apartheid state, from the Mediterranean to the Jordan. The reality we have now is the inevitable outcome of political Zionism and Jewish colonial settlement of Palestine, ok? And the peace process is a complete sham. It's not even a sham, the peace process is political theater to keep the process going of ridding the territory of non-Jews or containing and disenfranchising them in some way.[69]

Mark Braverman, 2013

The Boycott Divestment and Sanctions movement is, in fact, a nonviolent movement; it seeks to use established legal means to achieve its goals; and it is, interestingly enough, the largest Palestinian civic movement at this time. That means that the largest Palestinian civic movement is a nonviolent one that justifies its actions through recourse to international law. Further, I want to underscore that this is also a movement whose stated core principles include the opposition to every form of racism, including both state-sponsored racism and anti-Semitism.[70]

Judith Butler, February 2013

The fear of international sanctions work. The time has come to encourage the international community to fight Israeli intransigence and pressure Israel to give up on the occupied territories and its residents, who lack a voice from the perspective of our democracy. The 'La Familia' government will surrender.[71]

Yitzhak Laor, February 2013

II.3 Zionism, Then and Now

They have acted shamefully; They have done abhorrent things. Yet they do not feel shame, They cannot be made to blush.

Jeremiah 8:12

I am not a Zionist because I do not believe that any exclusively Jewish salvation program, in and of itself, can be permanently beneficial to Jewish life for the Jew is inseparably a part of civilization…Zionism offers neither a practical nor a spiritual solution to the Jewish problem, and indeed it can offer neither. For the "Jewish problem" is not really Jewish at all, though the Zionist is well on his way to making it so by seeking this thoroughgoing exclusiveness of Jewish life. The destiny oof the Jew still lies with the destiny of the liberal world. Because fundamentally, Zionism has no faith with that world, I am a non-Zionist.[72]

Rabbi Elmer Berger, 1943

[W]e must look squarely and honestly at the process of displacement that lies at the very root of Zionism's attempt to wrest the Land of Israel from its Palestinian inhabitants.[73]

Jeff Halper, 2008

It did not occur to me—so little did I know about the Middle East—that the establishment of a Jewish state meant the dispossession of the Arab majority that lived on that land. I was as ignorant of that as, when in school, I was shown a classroom map of American 'Western Expansion' and I assumed the white settlers were moving into empty territory. In neither case did I grasp that the advance of 'civilization' involved what we would today call 'ethnic cleansing.'

It was only after the 'Six-Day War' of 1967 and Israel's occupation of territories seized in that war (the West Bank, the Gaza Strip, the Golan Heights, and the Sinai peninsula) that I began to see Israel not simply as a beleaguered little nation surrounded by hostile Arab states, but as an expansionist power.

[...]

I have for a long time considered the nation-state as an abomination of our time [...] So for Jews to become another nation state, with all the characteristics of a nation-state—xenophobia, militarism, expansionism—never seemed to me a welcome development. And the policies of the State of Israel since its birth have borne out my fears. Some of the wisest Jews of our time—Einstein, Martin Buber—warned of the consequences of the Jewish state.[74]

Howard Zinn, 2008

Particularly in the younger generations, fewer and fewer American Jewish liberals are Zionists; fewer and fewer American Jewish Zionists are liberal. One reason is that the leading institutions of American Jewry have refused to foster—indeed, have actively opposed—a Zionism that challenges Israel's behavior in the West Bank and Gaza Strip and toward its own Arab citizens. For several decades, the Jewish establishment has asked American Jews to check their liberalism at Zionism's door, and now, to their horror, they are finding that many young Jews have checked their Zionism instead.[75]

Peter Beinart, May 12, 2010

Zionism, at its core, is a discriminatory ethnic nationalism that privileges the rights of Jews over non-Jews. [...] This is not an issue of 'warts' that need correction; this is an issue of systemic discrimination perpetrated in the name of the Jewish state and the Jewish people. There is no such thing as a democratic Jewish state. A Jewish state by definition cannot be democratic. As many in Israel say, Israel is a democratic state for Jews and a Jewish state for non-Jews.[76]

Rabbi Brian Walt, 2011

I grew up believing that Israel was the key to Jewish survival. But I would suggest that preserving Zionism is not the challenge facing Jews today. Rather, our task is to rescue Judaism from an ideology that has hijacked the faith, continues to fuel global conflict, and has produced one of the most systematic and longstanding violations of human rights in the world today. Despite its romantic attachment to the idea of the 'new Jew'—a Jew liberated from the powerlessness and humiliation of the ghetto—in reality Zionism has served to keep Jews trapped in an isolationist, exclusivist past. We must challenge a historical narrative that has yoked us to a theology of territoriality and tribal privilege.[77]

Mark Braverman, 2011

Zionism remains a deeply ethnocratic movement premised on a self-constructed narrative of 'historic right' to the entire 'promised land' (Palestine/Eretz Israel) and on the associated othering and dispossession of the Palestinians who object to the exclusivity of that right. This makes most Jews unable to deal with the core issues of the conflict, such as Israel's role in the Nakba—which remains the Archimedean point on which the Israeli regime is constructed. Denial of the Nakba becomes the cornerstone of Israeli ethnocracy. By justifying ethnic cleansing and the destruction of over four hundred Palestinian villages and towns, this denial has become a core Zionist value, fueling the 'right' of Jews to continue to colonize Palestine.[78]

Oren Yiftachel, 2012

When Zionism becomes coextensive with Jewishness, Jewishness is pitted against the diversity that defines democracy, and if I may say so, betrays one of the most important ethical dimensions of the diasporic Jewish tradition, namely, the obligation of cohabitation with those different from ourselves. Indeed, such a conflation denies the Jewish role in broad alliances in the historical struggle for social and political justice in unions, political demands for free speech, in socialist communities, in the resistance movement in World War II, in peace activism, the Civil Rights movement and the struggle against apartheid in South Africa.[79]

Judith Butler, 2013

Real liberal Zionists in Israel are dissatisfied with Israel's ethnic exclusivism, just as real liberals in America were dissatisfied with slavery, segregation, and institutionalized discrimination.[80]

Jerry Haber, 2013

Zionism proposed a Jewish state in Palestine as a solution to the great crisis of European Jewry in the late 19th and early 20th centuries. The Jewish state would protect a beleaguered people, end anti-Semitism and provide modern expression for Jewish nationalism. More than a century later, Israeli leaders, whether they believe in it or not, still invoke Zionism to justify their policies and to reject criticism. But the assumptions and beliefs that were an effective basis for policy a century ago are outlandish now.[81]

Ian Lustick, 2013

The Arabs might never accept the moral justice of Zionism, but, as the Arab Peace Initiative indicates, they would consider accepting the political legitimacy of a Jewish state. [...] Not even Israel's staunchest allies will risk an indefinite confrontation with the entire international community by supporting Israel's territorial ambitions. Reasonable border modifications are one thing; legitimizing a Jewish empire is quite another.[82]

Shlomo Ben-Ami, 2013

I identified Zionism as a kind of national liberation movement of the Jewish people. [...] Zionism has been for decades now the civil religion of American Jews.[83]

Rabbi Brant Rosen, 2013

II.4 Nonviolent Activism

Not by might, nor by power, but by my Spirit says the Lord.
Zechariah 4:6

The IDF is not a 'defense' force. It is an illegal occupying army that is brutalizing the Palestinian people. Why am I marching with 22 organizations to protest the Friends of the IDF dinner and the war criminal it is honoring? Quite simply: How could I not?[84]

Donna Nevel, 2010

We are a boat of the European Jewish organization Jews for Justice for Palestinians. We are on our way to Gaza. We are not armed and we believe in non-violence. And we are determined to proceed to the port of Gaza. You are imposing an illegal blockade on occupied Gaza. These are international waters and we do not recognize your authority here.

There are activists of all ages on this boat. Among us are Holocaust survivors, bereaved parents and Israelis who refuse to reconcile themselves to the illegal occupation of the Palestinian territories. We are unarmed peace activists who believe in nonviolence and we are determined to proceed on our way to the port of Gaza. We appeal to you, officers and soldiers of the IDF, to refuse and not to obey your commanders' illegal orders. For your information, the blockade of Gaza is illegal under international law and therefore you are running the risk of being put on trial at the international court for war crimes. The blockade and the occupation are inhumane and counter to universal morality and the values of Judaism. Use your consciences! Do not say 'I was only following orders!' Remember the painful story of our people! Refuse to enforce the blockade! Refuse the Occupation![85]

Yonatan Shapira, 2010

Fifty years ago next month, my father, then a 35-year-old refugee from Hitler's Germany with a young wife and two small children at home, boarded a Trailways bus headed for Jackson, Mississippi. [...] As we mark the 50th anniversary of those historic bus rides, a modern-day Freedom Ride will set out this June to challenge and focus international attention on another enduring and yet urgent injustice. The Israeli siege of Gaza has rendered 1.6 million souls—mostly refugees and the children and grandchildren of refugees—forgotten mates in the world's largest open-air prison. When the U.S. Boat to Gaza heads for Occupied Palestine, its passengers will not be guaranteed safe passage by any government. They will have no more assurance of success than did my father when he stepped onto that Trailways bus a half century ago. They will be armed only with a legacy of the courage of their activist forebears, the moral outrage of a growing worldwide movement for freedom and justice in Palestine, and the steadfast hopes of an illegally occupied people. They will be reasserting their faith in the validity—indeed the necessity—of a moral act.[86]

Hannah Schwarzschild, 2011

You are being told that action against the occupation will estrange you from the Jewish people. But the occupation is fundamentally contrary to our shared values of equality and justice. There is nothing Jewish about racial profiling with Hewlett Packard bio scanners. There is nothing Jewish about protecting stolen land with Motorola technology. There is nothing Jewish about demolishing Palestinian homes with Caterpillar bulldozers. [...] Right now, the Palestinians are not asking for you to invest in their economy. They are asking you to stop investing in and profiting from their suffering. They are asking you to engage in divestment, a time-tested, nonviolent, faithful act of love. Giving charity can also be loving. But dismissing Palestinian voices is not loving. [...] It's patronizing. If you truly want to help the Palestinian people, I urge you to listen to what they are asking for.[87]

Anna Baltzer, 2012

II.4 Nonviolent Activism

I began thinking about refusing to be conscripted into the Israeli Army during the 'Cast Lead' operation in 2008. The wave of aggressive militarism that swept the country then, the expressions of mutual hatred, and the vacuous talk about stamping out terror and creating a deterrent effect were the primary trigger for my refusal. Today, after four years full of terror, without a political process [towards peace negotiations], and without quiet in Gaza and Sderot, it is clear that the Netanyahu government, like that of his predecessor Olmert, is not interested in finding a solution to the existing situation, but rather in preserving it. From their point of view, there is nothing wrong with our initiating a 'Cast Lead 2' operation every three or four years (and then 3, 4, 5 and 6): we will talk of deterrence, we will kill some terrorists, we will lose some civilians on both sides, and we will prepare the ground for a new generation full of hatred on both sides. As representatives of the people, members of the cabinet have no duty to present their vision for the futures of the country, and they can continue with this bloody cycle, with no end in sight. But we, as citizens and human beings, have a moral duty to refuse to participate in this cynical game.[88]

Natan Blanc, 2012

It took the people of Nabi Saleh more than a year to get themselves organized. In December 2009 they held their first march, protesting not just the loss of the spring but also the entire complex system of control—of permits, checkpoints, walls, prisons—through which Israel maintains its hold on the region. Nabi Saleh quickly became the most spirited of the dozen or so West Bank villages that hold weekly demonstrations against the Israeli occupation. Since the demonstrations began, more than 100 people in the village have been jailed. Nariman told me that by her count, as of February, clashes with the army have caused 432 injuries, more than half to minors. The momentum has been hard to maintain—the weeks go by, and nothing changes for the better—but still, despite the arrests, the injuries and the deaths, every Friday after the midday prayer, the villagers, joined at times by equal numbers of journalists and Israeli and foreign activists, try to march from the center of town to the spring, a distance of perhaps half a mile. And every Friday, Israeli soldiers stop them with some combination of tear gas, rubber-coated bullets, water-cannon blasts of a noxious liquid known as 'skunk' and occasionally live fire. [...] The strategy appeared to work. After 55 demonstrations, the Israeli government agreed to shift the route of the barrier to the so-called 1967 green line.

The tactic spread to other villages: Biddu, Ni'lin, Al Ma'asara and in 2009, Nabi Saleh. Together they formed what is known as the 'popular resistance,' a loosely coordinated effort that has maintained what has arguably been the only form of active and organized resistance to the Israeli presence in the West Bank since the end of the second intifada in 2005. Nabi Saleh, Bassem hoped, could model a form of resistance for the rest of the West Bank. The goal was to demonstrate that it was still possible to struggle and to do so without taking up arms, so that when the spark came, if it came, resistance might spread as it had during the first intifada. 'If there is a third intifada,' he said, 'we want to be the ones who started it.'[89]

Ben Ehrenreich, 2013

I will tell you about one experience from that time. Spring 1942. I was a courier for an underground operation. I arrived to visit my friend from the youth movement, Dror Bachrubishov, in occupied eastern Poland very close to the Nazis. [...] The [Warsaw Ghetto] rebellion became for us [at that moment] necessary and clear. [...] Rebel against the Occupation. No—it is forbidden for us to rule over another people, to oppress another [people]. The most important thing is to achieve peace and an end to the cycle of blood[letting]. My generation dreamed of peace. I so want to achieve it. You have the power to help. All my hopes are with you.[90]

Chavka Fulman-Raban, 2013

Throwing stones is the birthright and duty of anyone subject to foreign rule. Throwing stones is an action as well as a metaphor of resistance. [...] Steadfastness (sumud) and resistance against the physical, and even more so the systemic, institutionalized violence, is the core sentence in the inner syntax of Palestinians in this land. This is reflected every day, every hour, every moment, without pause. [...] But on both sides of the Green Line, the levels of distress, suffocation, bitterness, anxiety and wrath are continually on the rise, as is the astonishment at Israelis' blindness in believing that their violence can remain in control forever.[91]

Amira Hass, 2013

By placing a billboard in Albany calling on the United States to end $30 billion of taxpayer-financed weapons to Israel, Stop $30 Billion–New York State is providing a valuable resource to people in New York, educating them about how our tax dollars could be better spent on unmet community needs rather than on enabling Israel's oppression of Palestinians.[92]

Noam Chomsky, 2013

II.5 As a Jew

If I am only for myself, who am I?
Rabbi Hillel, Pirkei Avot 1:14

I don't buy the rationalizations any more. I'm so tired of the apologetics. How on earth will squeezing the life out of Gaza, not to mention bombing the living hell out of it, ensure the safety of Israeli citizens? We good liberal Jews are ready to protest oppression and human rights abuse anywhere in the world, but are all too willing to give Israel a pass. It's a fascinating double standard, and one I understand all too well. I understand it because I've been just as responsible as anyone else for perpetrating it. So no more rationalizations. What Israel has been doing to the people of Gaza is an outrage. It has brought neither safety nor security to the people of Israel and it has wrought nothing but misery and tragedy upon the people of Gaza. There, I've said it. Now what do I do?[93]

Rabbi Brant Rosen, 2008

But it has become progressively more difficult in recent years for those who call themselves 'liberals' to defend Israeli conduct. The Gaza invasion marked the climax of Israel's incremental descent into barbarism.[94]

Norman G. Finkelstein, 2010

The most effective way for progressive Jews to promote change in Israel, is by building a grassroots, interfaith American movement that calls on our government to promote a just solution to the conflict that grants equal human rights to all who live in Israel/Palestine.[95]

Rabbi Brian Walt, 2011

I would argue that an honest analysis of the situation shows that mainstream Jewish American institutions are among the traditional gatekeepers on this issue, and Jewish voices are uniquely placed to challenge and disrupt those institutions' hegemony. We must be present in coalitions challenging those institutions, defending allies from claims of anti-Semitism that are used to stifle legitimate discussion about Israel and to suppress action. The more of us that speak out, the harder it becomes for pro-occupation Jewish institutions to claim to be in any way representative. By showing that the Jewish community is not monolithic, we show that this is not an identity-based struggle between Jews and Palestinians but a struggle for human rights like any other. [...]

Historically, the role of Jewish American allies has been to show that it's okay to criticize Israel, to support boycott and divestment, etc. But what's really needed is a complete paradigm shift; it's the concept that you, whoever you are, do not need permission from Jews—or anyone else for that matter—to do what you believe is the right thing to do.[96]

Anna Baltzer, 2012

[G]rassroots activists, joining together as part of an international movement, are developing a new discourse which is human rights-based, rather than focused on Jewish victimhood and exceptionalism at the expense of the Palestinian population.[97]

Alice Rothchild, 2013

[T]he cornerstone value of my religious tradition commands me to stand in solidarity with all who are oppressed. It would be a profound betrayal of my own Jewish heritage if I consciously choose not to stand with the Palestine people. [...] I believe my Jewish liberation to be intrinsically bound up with Palestinian liberation. It's really that simple.[98]

Rabbi Brant Rosen, 2013

II.5 As a Jew

That feeling of living in a society where culture is dominant is for many of us if not most of us [Jews] in the United States really pretty seductive because it's not something that we experience here. At the same time I can't justify to myself the oppression of another people for the sake of that feeling. There's no getting around the fact that Israel is based on a system of ethnic supremacy, and that what kind of life you can lead there is largely determined by whether you are Jewish or not.[99]

Rebecca Vilkomerson, 2013

'I love Israel' isn't a Jewish credential. It impedes our ability to think.[100]

Marc Ellis, 2013

A lot of my initial activism on this issue involved Jewish handwringing: workshops about the Jewish family and trauma and our inhibitions about speaking our minds and hurting our parents, all because we were looking into the Nakba and uttering phrases like, equal rights. Given that so many activists had to go through this process before they could be clear and effective, I imagine the official Jewish community is now embarking on its own handwringing interlude—in which it discovers the Nakba and doesn't know what to do about it.[101]

Philip Weiss, 2013

My personal reasons for joining this movement for justice as a Jew, i.e. Jewish values, are not to be confused with my activism in the movement itself, which is based upon acting in solidarity with Palestinians. As a non-Zionist, I feel no inherent connection to Israel. As a Jew, that connection is not required.[102]

Heike Schotten, 2013

II.6 Antisemitism and Interfaith Relations

It is not incumbent upon you to complete the work; but neither are you free to desist from it.

Pirkei Avot 2:21

The answer to anti-Semitism, a compelling concern of Zionism, is not a militarily strong Israel embroiled in an intractable conflict that carries the danger of escalating into a genuine and irresolvable 'clash of civilizations' involving Jews everywhere. Rather, it is a world based on human rights in which anti-Semitism is opposed like any other form of racism. [...] Israel is not the ultimate protector of Jewish life; human rights are.[103]

Jeff Halper, 2008

Sixty five years ago, the Christian world stood before the ovens of Auschwitz-Birkenau and said, 'What have we done?' Since then, Christian-Jewish relations have been driven by the Jewish desire for safety and protection on the one hand and the powerful Christian drive for penitence for millennia of anti-Jewish doctrine and behavior on the other.

For Jews, the establishment of the State of Israel has provided the focus of this quest for physical security, dignity, and self-determination. For their part, Christians set about developing a revised theology that renounced the notion that Christians had replaced the Jewish people as God's chosen and that granted implicit and in many cases explicit theological justification for political Zionism.

The result is that Christian-Jewish 'interfaith' relations today follows clear rules—rules that serve to insulate Christians from any appearance of anti-Jewish feeling and that protect the Jewish community from any possible challenge—or even perceived challenge—to unconditional support for the policies of the State of Israel. These rules are playing out in the academy, in the pews, in interfaith relations on the highest levels, and in everyday encounters. They are rendered more powerful by never being stated or acknowledged.[104]

Mark Braverman, 2010

Christians in America [...] adopted the conviction that, after the Holocaust, Israel was essential to Jewish survival and flourishing. Christians also came to believe that support for the State of Israel was part of Christian repentance for their historic sin of anti-Semitism. In some quarters, Holocaust theology became so pervasive that it became difficult to ascertain whether it was more important to Jews or Christians.[105]

Marc Ellis, 2012

The bad conscience of Zionism cannot distinguish between authentic criticism and the mirrored delusions of anti-Semitism lying ready-made in the swamps of our civilization and awakened by the current crisis. Both are threats, though the progressive critique is more telling, as it contests the concrete reality of Israel and points toward self-transformation by differentiating Jewishness from Zionism; while anti-Semitism regards the Jew abstractly and in a demonic form, as 'Jewish money' or 'Jewish conspiracies,' and misses the real mark. Indeed, Zionism makes instrumental use of anti-Semitism, as a garbage pail into which all opposition can be thrown, and a germinator of fearfulness around which to rally Jews. This is not to discount the menace posed by anti-Semitism nor the need to struggle vigorously against it. But the greater need is to develop a genuinely critical perspective, and not be bullied into confusing critique of Israel with anti-Semitism. One cannot in conscience condemn anti-Semitism by rallying around Israel, when it is Israel that needs to be fundamentally changed if the world is to awaken from this nightmare.[106]

Joel Kovel, 2013

I conclude, then, that the very idea of a Jewish state is undemocratic, a violation of the self-determination rights of its non-Jewish citizens, and therefore morally problematic. [...] There is an unavoidable conflict between being a Jewish state and a democratic state. I want to emphasize that there's nothing anti-Semitic in pointing this out, and it's time the question was discussed openly on its merits, without the charge of anti-Semitism hovering in the background.[107]

Joseph Levine, 2013

An olive tree stands in front of the Separation Wall near the Bethlehem checkpoint on 2 February 2009. During the construction of the Wall, tens of thousands of olive trees have been destroyed. The route of the Wall was declared illegal by the International Court of Justice in 2005. Photo by: Anne Paq. Activestills Photo Collective, all rights reserved.

III. ENGAGING JEWISH VOICES OF CONSCIENCE AND DISSENT, POST 7 OCTOBER 2023

Introduction

"Justice, justice, ye shall pursue justice." (Deuteronomy 16:20) Justice and equal rights for all people are the essence of Judaism. Despite its establishment as a Jewish state in 1948, these values were neither reflected in political Zionism then nor evidenced since in the laws and practices of the state of Israel.

Considering ways to think about the unthinkable in the aftermath of 7 October 23, I instinctively began collecting clear thoughtful commentary from respected Jewish sources: scholars, historians, theologians, journalists, and investigative reporters. Reflecting on my two previous booklets, I wondered aloud with friends, what was the contribution they made, and how did they accomplish whatever that was? We agreed that they offered a contextual understanding of the present, perhaps even as an inevitable consequence of the past. In that lightbulb moment, I recognized it was time for this book to be written.

Gaza has its own story. The population of Gaza is predominantly first, second, and now third generation refugees of the Nakba. The 140 square miles of the Gaza Strip were not conquered in 1948. Of the 750,000 indigenous Palestinians who were displaced in 1948 from the land in historic Palestine on which their families had been living for generations, 250,000 were forced into Gaza.

Gaza became isolated from the rest of Palestine after the 1948 war. The armistice line separating the Gaza Strip from Palestinian lands seized by Israel in 1948 became the site of resistance to ongoing domination, dehumanization, and military incursions that accompany colonial rule. Once a thriving agricultural and trade hub with fields of barley, wheat, and orange groves, Gaza suffered a devastating economic collapse. Restrictions on the activities of daily life and movement further intensified in 2007 when Israel imposed a siege on Gaza, enforcing a blockade of goods and people in and out of the Gaza Strip. Given its size, the population density, poverty, and brutal occupation, life in Gaza was deemed unsustainable.

The response by Gazans to this systemic cruelty and oppression has included decades of civil disobedience, nonviolent protest, diplomacy, armed struggle, and unarmed mass mobilization, only to be met by increased Israeli violence, repression, and dismissal of their demands. As the Israeli government moved further and further to the far-right, strategies of forced transfer or annihilation were actively considered. By 2023, any concern other Arab countries had for Palestine was superseded by efforts to normalize relations with Israel, closing the door on support for equality, freedom, and basic human rights for Palestinians. The subsequent explosion of violence between the river and the sea was described in 2025 by Jehad Abusalim, Executive Director of the Institute for Palestine Studies, as an "existential reckoning" for Palestinians.[108]

Archival documents describing the establishment of a Jewish homeland in historic Palestine disclose forethought and intention to rid the land of its indigenous population. As the story has been told over decades, Israel wanted all the land and none of the people. The Hamas attack on 7 October presented both pretext and opportunity for Zionism to achieve its founding objective through the evisceration of the Gaza Strip. Consider Israel's indiscriminate and disproportionate bombing, refusal to sustain a negotiated ceasefire, wanton destruction of Gaza's infrastructure, withholding food, flour, water, and humanitarian aid, targeted assassinations of physicians, educators, aid workers, and journalists, and a civilian death toll that exceeds proportionality and is consistent with the goal of erasure.

The regional and global impact of the war on Gaza appears to be changing the politics, geography, and people of the region in ways not yet known. Israel's alliance with US hegemony factors into the seemingly irreparable political fracturing of familial and communal relationships, as well as intensifying competing national loyalties.

And yet, as the world is haunted by the threat of fascism, Palestinians steadfastly refuse to be disappeared by powers that deface, destroy, dehumanize, and attempt to erase the entirety of this indigenous people.

In *Part Three*, often-neglected critical distinctions between Judaism and Zionism come into clear focus, shattering the conflation of Judaism as a religion with Zionism as an ideology, and disputing longstanding omissions, myths, propaganda, and confusion regarding Israeli statehood and Palestinian dispossession. Real time responses to 7 October 2023 inform and inspire a radical rethinking on several ever-expanding fronts. While the Hamas attack and Palestinian struggle have little to do with hatred of Jews, antisemitism has become a wedge issue to deflect from the war on Gaza and to deny the legitimate demands of Palestinians. This political quicksand endangers everyone, as it repurposes a disingenuous desire to protect Jews with a growing authoritarian control of both free speech and a wide range of progressive political agendas. It is not only Palestine that is threatened with erasure.

Safety doesn't come from supremacy, guns, checkpoints, walls, and a police state. Safety is built through forging real solidarity with others standing together to build a world where all people can live in freedom, safety, and equality.

In this precarious turning point moment, Part Three lifts accounts of witness and truth. As Israel unrelentingly commits a plausible genocide in Gaza and the West Bank, the time-honored tradition of Jewish dissent to nationalism, militarism, supremacy, and hubris provides a moral compass. Dissent disrupts interlinking systemic oppression and injustice. Truth-telling is an act of conscience, also known as teshuvah, a turning. This final section highlights the vital roles of conscience and dissent in animating responsible individual and collective actions.

Susan Landau, December 2024

III.1 Initial Responses: In the Aftermath of 7 October 2023

> *Justice, not revenge, is the way. The lesson of the Holocaust is to end the cycle of violence and atrocity. There is no other way.*[109]
>
> Marc Ellis, 2002

While the sheer scope of our grief may feel incomprehensible, we simply must find the wherewithal to say out loud that the facts of these events have not only been comprehensible, but in fact inevitable.

Indeed, Palestinians and their allies have long been sounding the alarm that Israel was subjecting Palestinians to a brutally violent apartheid regime against Palestinians with impunity—and there would be terrible consequences if the international community failed to intervene. Over and over, we've been warned about the cataclysmic violence that would inevitably ensue if Israel was not held to account. As Palestinian historian Rashid Khalidi put it recently, 'an entire people (has been) living under this kind of incredible oppression, in a pressure cooker. It had to explode.' […]

[Though] it may seem more painfully difficult than ever, let us hearken to [these] voices that have so long been crying out from the ground. Let us respond with understanding, compassion and action. Even amidst the terrible grief, let us shine an unflinching light on the true roots of this violence—and on the vision of a future based on justice and equality for all who live in the land.[110]

Rabbi Brant Rosen, October 12, 2023

In October 1973, and again in October 2023, Israel suffered a breakdown in political and military command. It could not have imagined that the Arabs were capable or courageous enough to launch such a daring attack. […]

It has been more than ten hours, and Israelis in settlements throughout the Naqab and especially around Gaza are under siege, with Palestinian fighters in control and only a small Israeli military presence. What is perhaps even harder to grasp is that Palestinian fighters have entered and now control the Gaza Brigade headquarters of the IDF—this is where the brigade commander, a general, is stationed. Palestinians from Gaza are walking freely around a military base in disbelief by deserted Israeli tanks. [...]

In the wars that preceded 1973, Israel always attacked when its enemies were weak and unprepared. In October 1973 and again in October 2023, Israelis got a taste of their own medicine. What's more, they fell apart militarily and politically.

One thing is certain: regardless of how successful this operation turns out, Palestinians are likely to pay a heavy price. [...] Hopefully, this Palestinian military success will lead to real political gain for all Palestinians.[111]

Miko Peled, October 7, 2023

Clearly, this act by Hamas is suicidal. It is an attack of unprecedented scope, and Israel will retaliate to a greater degree than it has before, potentially leading to outcomes we haven't seen before: not just a simple razing of Gaza by airplanes but also a ground incursion and potential reoccupation of parts of Gaza. So the decision to wittingly, knowingly, undertake this comes from a sense that there are no other options and that there's nothing left to lose. And part of the reason that Hamas, and Palestinians in general, feel that they're in such a desperate situation is that they have been entirely abandoned by those who should be their allies. [...]

It's hard to overstate how shocking these images are to the Israeli public. Gaza is made up of refugees from towns within Israel, and more than seventy per cent of the population of Gaza comprises refugees, so it's something out of Israeli nightmares that the refugees are going to come storming back and take over their old towns.

That degree of shock and that degree of military failure by Israel— not simply that the attack took place but that you and I are talking now, more than twelve hours after it occurred, and reports are that Hamas fighters have taken over and are still controlling military bases outside Gaza— is incomprehensible to any Israeli. Politically, it is hard to imagine that this government will not feel a need to exact an extraordinary price in order to save face.[112]

Nathan Thrall, October 8, 2023

[W]ill you be able to learn the other important lesson – one that can be gleaned from recent events – that sheer force alone cannot find the balance between a just regime on the one hand and an immoral political project on the other?

But there is an alternative. In fact, there has always been one:

A de-zionised, liberated and democratic Palestine from the river to the sea; a Palestine that will welcome back the refugees and build a society that does not discriminate on the basis of culture, religion or ethnicity.[113]

Ilan Pappé, October 10, 2023

Part of what has made the experience of this event feel so different from the status quo—and so different to Palestinians and Jews—comes from the fact that Palestinians were undeniably the actors, for once, not the acted upon. The protagonists of the story. I consider it an enormous failure of our movements that we have not been able to build a vehicle for that kind of reversal in any other way thus far. Our Jewish movements for Palestine were not powerful enough to stop other Jews from gunning down Palestinians in peaceful marches at the Gazan border fence, or to keep Palestinians from being fired, harassed, and sued for speaking the truth about their experience or—God forbid—advocating the nonviolent tactic of boycott. And now, we do not have a shared struggle able to credibly respond to these massacres of Israelis and Palestinians. With all of the work that many Jews and Palestinians have done to reach toward each other over the years, I believe at heart it is this failure that is now driving us apart. There is no formidable political formation that I know of that can hold the political subjectivity of both Jews and Palestinians in this moment without simply attempting to assimilate one into the other. No place where Jews and Palestinians who agree on the basics of Palestinian liberation—right of return, equality, and reparations—are poised to turn the synthesis of these two subjectivities into a coherent strategy.

One of the most terrible things about this event is the sense of its inevitability. The violence of apartheid and colonialism begets more violence. Many people have struggled with the straitjacket of this inevitability, straining to articulate that its recognition does not mean its embrace. I am reminding myself that it was from Palestinians, many of them writing and speaking in these pages, that I learned to think of Palestine as a site of possibility—a place where the very idea of the nation-state, which has so harmed both peoples, could be remade or destroyed entirely. And it was Palestinians who opened my thinking to multiple visions of sharing the land. On the left, I hope we do not mistake the inevitability of the violence for an inescapable limit on our work or the quality of our thought. Even if our dreams for better have failed, they must accompany us through this moment to the other side. We need to imagine a movement for liberation better even than the Exodus—an exodus where neither people has to leave. Where people stay to pick up the pieces, rearranging themselves not just as Jews or Palestinians but as antifascists and workers and artists. I want what Puerto Rican Jewish poet and activist Aurora Levins Morales describes in her poem 'Red Sea':

> We cannot cross until we carry each other,
> all of us refugees, all of us prophets.
> No more taking turns on history's wheel,
> trying to collect old debts no-one can pay.
> The sea will not open that way.
> our rage pressed cheek to cheek
> until tears flood the space between,
> until there are no enemies left,
> because this time no one will be left to drown
> and all of us must be chosen.
> This time it's all of us or none.
> This time that country
> is what we promise each other,
>
> our rage pressed cheek to cheek
>
> until tears flood the space between,
>
> until there are no enemies left,
>
> because this time no one will be left to drown
>
> and all of us must be chosen.
>
> This time it's all of us or none.[114]

Arielle Angel, October 12, 2023

The Israeli attacks constitute an arrogant insanity layered with racism, Islamophobia, and vengeance. Their stated concern for civilians is not remotely credible. And when it is over, who will emerge as the next leaders of Palestine? After years of post-Oslo dialogue and concessions that have only produced more losses of land, dehumanization, humiliation, death, and hopelessness, Israelis are not safer and Palestinians still call for their human and civil rights, a recognition of their humanity, and repair and reparations for their decades of ongoing trauma. Once again, the Israel government seems to have no end game besides maximum death and destruction. This is madness.[115]

Alice Rothchild, October 14, 2023

This is not the time to root for your team. This is the time to stand on the side of humanity. To protect civilians. To imagine a future when Israelis and Palestinians both live in safety and with dignity.

This past Yom Kippur, when the recent attack by Hamas was unimagined, I gave a sermon about Israel and said the following:

> On Yom Kippur, we take time to consider our ideals, and visions, and the narratives that shaped us. We take stock of who we are, and of what we believe. We ask ourselves whether the stories of our past still speak to the actual world we live in. We ask ourselves whether our political beliefs are aligned with our values. We ask ourselves, in what way will we engage and speak out?
>
> I believe that Israel is the most important moral issue of the Jewish people in this era. What happens in the next ten or twenty years will profoundly affect the future of Jews, Judaism, and Jewish life.
>
> My core values are democracy, equality, human rights and civil rights. I think it's important to articulate them over and over again. I don't want to practice a version of Judaism, or be part of a Jewish community, that sidelines or stifles them.

At this time of war, I stand by these words. Now is the time to embrace our deepest values and protest this bloodshed.[116]

Rabbi Laurie Zimmerman, October 16, 2023

We are Rabbis and Rabbinical students and at this moment of great moral reckoning, we are speaking out with one voice.

Those of us grieving both Israeli and Palestinian loved ones this week know there is no military solution to our horror. [...]

In the face of this terrifying, violence, we say no!

We uplift the Torah value of v'chai bahem– live by Torah. Torah should be a source of life, not death.

As Jews, as Rabbis, as human beings we are pleading with our communities to rise through our despair and our grief to save lives.

As Americans, we call upon our leaders to stop supporting and enabling this nightmare

We call upon all Americans to call their representatives and demand that they act immediately

Our tradition is an Eytz Hayim – a tree of life. Life, not death, are its fruits.

We ask you to join our calls for a complete ceasefire now. [...]

Ceasefire is the only way to prevent more death and destruction.

All human beings are made b'tzelem Elohim – in the image of the Divine. All human life is sacred and precious.

Too many precious lives are being killed.

The voice of the Jewish people, now more than ever, must be clear and united:

Never Again is Now.

Never again for anyone.

Not in our names.

Ceasefire now![117]

Rabbis for Ceasefire, October 20, 2023

III.2 Considering the Context: Settler Colonialism, Supremacy, and Hubris

Acknowledging the past is the first step in coming to terms with its consequences.[118]
Zochrot

A settler-colonial project is one in which a group of persecuted white Europeans flee Europe to colonize a place in order to make it their homeland. The colonists view native populations as an impediment to their goals and as such treat them poorly. [...]
   Whereas the remedy for *colonialism* is to send the colonial power and largely its settlers' home, the remedy for the abuses that take place in a *settler* colonial project is the application of equal rights.[119]

Rabbi Shai Gluskin, October 29, 2018

The political economy of settler colonialism differs from other colonial contexts in that for settlers, the goal is *not* the exploitation of indigenous labor, but the expropriation of indigenous land.[120]

Joseph Francis Getzoff, July 2020

The events of October 7 have reminded us that resistance to settler colonialism is ever-present. The only way forward is decolonization, and that requires us to foreground a political solution. [...]
   It is not a 'conflict.' There are no 'sides,' no symmetry of 'violence.' The settler project is a unilateral one that must deny the indigenous

population's existence as a people endowed with rights to their land and identities if it is to claim the country exclusively for itself. [...]

The colonial structures of domination and control must be thoroughly dismantled. [...] An anti-colonial struggle can engender only one post-colonial reality: liberation, the restoration of the national rights of the colonized, and, in the case of the Palestinians, the return of the refugees. [...]

But only the establishment of a common civil state of equal citizens [...] will be able to cope with the complex post-colonial process of constructing a new, shared state and civil society.[121]

Jeff Halper, October 20, 2023

In 1831, a slave named Nat Turner organized an insurrection in Virginia. It proved to be the largest slave revolt in American history. [...] It's unknown whether Turner expected to achieve a military victory or, short of that, force a national reckoning with slavery. [...] The unfolding scene was ghastly. [...]

Turner was demonized by Whites after his death, the honorable exception being the White Abolitionists. [...] Even as none contested the gruesome facts of the rebellion, southern Blacks did not recoil in horror at Turner's name. [...] By now, Nat Turner occupies an honored place in American history.

The 2,000 young men who burst the gates of Gaza on October 7, 2023, had been born into a concentration camp. For fully two decades they had been immured in a 25-mile long by 5-mile-wide sliver of land that was among the most densely populated places in the world. The vast majority of them could never hope to leave but only to pace each day the camp's suffocating perimeter; never aspire to gainful employment or eat a full meal; never expect to marry or raise a family. Abandoned by everyone, they were 'remaindered' to languish and die. To expedite this process, Israel periodically launched 'operations' visiting death and destruction on Gaza: thousands methodically mowed down; homes and critical infrastructure systematically pulverized. It might sound like the script of a bad B-movie, but on the night of October 6 each of those 2,000 men probably kissed his mother, then his father, goodbye. Forever. And then each silently vowed to vindicate the remorseless torture of a twilight existence, and to avenge the murder of a grandparent, sister, brother, niece, nephew by that Satanic power that cursed their lives. [...]

It's still high noon and thus too soon to resolve what verdict History will cast on the slave revolt in Gaza on October 7, 2023.[122]

Norman Finkelstein, October 26, 2023

For too long the discourse and understanding in this country was dominated by one side imbued with Zionism.

In 1984, Edward Said called out this dynamic and demanded that Palestinians have the Permission to Narrate their existence. He did not just mean the ability for Palestinians to tell their own stories, but to hold agency over their lives. This is the power of truth telling. And this power has been seen in Gaza. [...]

[S]ometimes those of us in the movement are more comfortable with the idea of Palestinians as victims than we are with Palestinians as agents of their own destiny. And October 7 was a monumental challenge to this worldview.

At its heart October 7 was a cry from Palestinians locked in the world's largest prison, besieged for 17 years, saying, 'We will not die silently. We will resist.' This is a message that I believe we need to engage and wrestle with.[123]

Adam Horowitz, March 22, 2024

Obviously, no victory has been achieved in Gaza and no victory will be achieved in Gaza. But if Israel needs the pretense in order to climb down the blood-soaked tree it has ascended, a tree it shouldn't have climbed in the first place, it's better to fake a victory. Hamas has sustained a military blow but has won in every other aspect. Israel has been routed diplomatically, socially, morally and economically. But let local media sing Israel's praises; it likes to engage in deception and tell you about the 'excellent work' the Israel Defense Forces is doing in the Gaza Strip.

Israel's situation at the end of the war is incalculably worse than it was at the start of its most redundant war. Not that there was no justification, but war is assessed by its results, and these were known in advance: pointlessly being bogged down, a shedding of Palestinian blood as though it were water, as well as the blood of many soldiers, the transformation of Israel into a pariah state, and all for nothing.[124]

Gideon Levy, Jun 23, 2024

Expulsion. Annexation. Siege. Massacre. Injustice layered on injustice, atrocity compounding atrocity, sedimented savagery amounting in sum to a colossal crime against humanity—culminating in the blockade and bombardment of a refugee population, confined in a concentration camp, *one-half of whom were children*. It would surprise if suffering of this severity were a recipe for long-term stability. Israeli officials [Military Intelligence chief Herzl Halevi] knew that the 'humanitarian condition in Gaza' was 'progressively deteriorating'—this being the intended outcome of Israeli policy—and could predict that, 'if it blows up, it'll be in Israel's direction.' But they apparently believed that [...] Palestinian eruptions could be contained within tolerable limits. Hamas will 'rise up from time to time and hit us,' Israel's former national security advisor acknowledged in 2018, but '[i]t can't cause us any real damage.' If the timing, scale, and character of the October 7 attack came as a shock, the fact that people in Gaza would strike out at some point and in some fashion was not just predictable but priced into Israel's 'conflict management' policy. Indeed, a former deputy to Israel's national security adviser found in the Hamas-led assault, not proof of Gazans' irrational barbarism, but confirmation of a historical universal: 'Eventually the oppressed will rise against their oppressor.'[125]

Jamie Stern-Weiner, 2023

It's becoming ominously clear that the end game of Israel's genocide in Gaza is the end of game of Zionism itself: namely, settlement. [...]

As a settler colonial movement, Zionism was always focused on the maintenance of a majority Jewish presence in historic Palestine. However, the seizing and control of resources has been no less integral to this project. The settler colonial reality of the 21st century is driven in no small part by the corporate interest of weapons manufacturers as well as the billionaire and oligarch class that seek to profit off the spoils of war and genocide. In the current moment, it should come as no surprise that there is also unabashed talk about the annexation of the West Bank and even parts of South Lebanon.

Such is the natural result of a movement and ideology that prizes real estate over the well-being of the actual people who happen to live on the land.[126]

Rabbi Brant Rosen, November 22, 2024

I think it [is] the beginning of the end of the Zionist project and people who are good historians will remind the readers that the beginning of an end of projects such as Zionism is the most dangerous in the history of a place. [...] The basic moral, [...] economic and military infrastructure that holds together the state of Israel and allows it to oppress the Palestinians is being eroded. [...] This is going to continue in the future. And there are all kinds of transformations in world public opinion, in the position of governments in the Global South, among the Jewish communities, that indicate that there is a good possibility for an alliance that would be more effective than in the past in helping Palestinians to obtain their goals of liberation, decolonization and survival.[127]

Ilan Pappé, March 7, 2024

III.3 Unbending the Arc: Genocide, Complicity, and Responsibility

We must continue to remind ourselves that in a free society all are involved in what some are doing. Some are guilty; all are responsible.[128]

Abraham Joshua Heschel, 1996

To be Jewish in a time of genocide means that you have a duty and a responsibility to speak up. The second that we start deciding that 'never again' means only 'never again' for some people, I think that we've lost the teachings from people who have survived genocide.[129]

Bella Jacobs, April 26, 2024

Israel's campaign to displace Gazans—and potentially expel them altogether into Egypt—is yet another chapter in the Nakba, in which an estimated 750,000 Palestinians were driven from their homes during the 1948 war that led to the creation of the State of Israel. But the assault on Gaza can also be understood in other terms: as a textbook case of genocide unfolding in front of our eyes. I say this as a scholar of genocide, who has spent many years writing about Israeli mass violence against Palestinians. I have written about settler colonialism and Jewish supremacy in Israel, the distortion of the Holocaust to boost the Israeli arms industry, the weaponization of antisemitism accusations to justify Israeli violence against Palestinians, and the racist regime of Israeli apartheid. Now, following Hamas's attack on Saturday and the mass murder of more than 1,000 Israeli civilians, the worst of the worst is happening.

Under international law, the crime of genocide is defined by 'the intent to destroy, in whole or in part, a national, ethnical, racial or religious group, as such,' as noted in the December 1948 UN Convention on the Prevention and Punishment of the Crime of Genocide. In its murderous attack on Gaza, Israel has loudly proclaimed this intent.[130]

Raz Segal, October 13, 2023

I think that we have a moral and, one could also argue, legal obligation to compare the Holocaust and the atrocities committed during the Second World War to the present. If we take the promise of never again seriously, we once again have to constantly be asking ourselves, are we laying the foundations for the mass murder of millions of people? Are we employing or is part of the world employing the same kinds of tactics that were employed by the Nazis? I think there's every reason to say that that is exactly what's happening.[131]

Masha Gessen, December 22, 2023

Israel is not the safest place for Jews. In fact, Israel is one of the most unsafe places for Jews and has been so for the last few decades. Because this is the place where there is constant violence, and it is built on the Palestinian Nakba of 1948. It is built on such a crime that it has to sustain violence in order to sustain itself. And that means it can never be safe, unless it is going through a process of decolonization and democratization.

Deep down, I think most Israeli Jews know that. [...]

This is about the fact that there are all these millions of people who are dispossessed, who are living on their land, and [Israel] cannot contain them. We will never be able to contain that because all people want to live in freedom. And that means that Israel can never be a safe haven for the Jews until it becomes safe for Palestinians.[132]

Dov Baum, 2023

III.3 Unbending the Arc: Genocide, Complicity, and Responsibility

It will take lifetimes to reclaim and try to recover from the devastation that has been unleashed on an entire people. We know what that's like. And it shows that we basically lost any innocence that we felt or any sense that we were going to be unscathed or that we were going to become righteous because we suffered so much. That is gone completely, and this will require the best of us in the future, people who are willing to overcome the past and to humbly courageously and with love develop a spiritual practice that allows for Teshuvah, atonement, for reparations, for guarantees of non-repeat, and to keep centering Palestinian lives as we continue the work of solidarity from this generation to the next.[133]

Rabbi Lynn Gottlieb, July 31, 2024

Four a.m. seems to be my witching hour, the time past which I cannot sleep. [...] Instead, I will reach for my phone. [...] In what feels like a version of Russian roulette, I will call upon WhatsApp to help me figure out if T's father is still alive in Gaza.

On Friday, October 13, T called me. When I answered I could hear only her sobs. *Breathe, habibti*, I told her. This was the day the Israelis issued their first go-South-or-else ultimatum to the people of Gaza City, where her father lived. He had just called to give her his email password so she could access his important documents and information, because he did not want to leave. She understood what this meant. She was inconsolable. I packed a few things and drove for two hours to be with her. While I was there, we managed a short WhatsApp video call with H. He asked about her studies and made a dad joke. He urged her not to worry. Then he ended the call the way he always did: Take care of your mom. I love you, baba.

[...]

If life is being uprooted from the land, where, then, does one look for it in Gaza?

Under the rubble.

People return, because they always return, to their smashed homes. Scrambling among the unsteady heaps, they retrieve what the cement and rebar will relinquish: a frying pan, a chair, schoolbooks, a favorite stuffed animal.

But the greatest prizes are retrieved by men in orange vests, the ash of their former city lodged permanently in their beards. They are the ones who pull children from the depths, like midwives birthing a new life. They spend hours calming these pockets of life found amidst mounds of death, encouraging their little ones to breathe – kudh nefes, habibi – as others, like cement surgeons, use saws, drills, and blood-stained hands to extract. Through the narrowest of openings, babies coated in dust and debris emerge, crouched and shivering, first slowly, deliberately, and then in one final energetic burst, to the cheers of their new family. They are washed in water from a plastic bottle; swaddled in a shirt. The bundle is then placed in someone's arm, and even in the dim light of a cell phone, one sees tears trace a path down his dust-covered cheeks. He rocks and coos and sings to soothe himself as much as the miracle in his arms.[134]

Alison Glick, February 24, 2024

Genocide is our hands, it has eaten our souls. Our flesh might have survived nazi Germany but our morality has been exterminated. This is the real Shoah of us and there is no surviving this. There are over a million people in Gaza who have been forcefully displaced. You live in their home. Next time that your soldier-kin calls to say their unit just left Gaza for a break and you cry tears of relief, I want you to get into a bathtub filled by the blood of all the children we have murdered in the last 75 years. Sit there until you are able to match each drop of blood with a tear. This might take generations. Only when the bathtub is filled with clear Salt Water, will you be washed.[135]

meital yaniv, 2023

As if any grief, however vast, however deep, down to the core of the Earth and up into the stars, could justify genocide. As if mourning, even thousands of years of mourning, somehow makes just children's bodies broken, dashed, shattered, scattered.

What are we if we can pretend our need to feel safe, to be safe, justifies colonization, occupation, imprisonment, mass murder?

My god how awful it is, how horrible beyond measure, how it breaks your heart open, that weeping for Zion has been swallowed whole by Zionism.[136]

Elliott batTzedek, February 15, 2024

Israelis' hearts are with the Israeli victims, it's human. But the overwhelming focus on six hostages versus the neglect of tens of thousands of Palestinian victims is sickening and immoral.

Israel mourns the six hostages who were killed. The world also mourns them. Their names, their pictures, their life stories and their families led news broadcasts in Israel and around the world. [...]

Their becoming a global story is understandable. Less understandable is the unbelievable contrast between the wide coverage of their lives and deaths and the total disregard for the similar fate of people their own age—as blameless and ingenuous and beautiful as them, and just as much innocent victims—on the Palestinian side.[137]

Gideon Levy, September 5, 2024

We should then not ask why the world condemns us, why Israeli lecturers are not allowed to lecture abroad, why the world does not want to trade with Israel or visit Israel, why all the 'good people' don't accept us and don't understand us. The actions being carried out today are evidently immoral acts that undermine the moral identity of the entire State of Israel and its citizens.

Many Israelis said after October 7 that all Gazans were guilty because they elected Hamas and were complicit in its rule. They said there were no innocents in Gaza because Gazans knew and kept quiet. In this respect, like the Gazans, we are all complicit.

None of this means that they or we deserve to starve to death, to be killed by a rocket, by a knife or by a bomb. But it does mean that we bear responsibility and that we must speak out against a government that makes us complicit against our will. [...]

We were slaves in Egypt – we should hope that this taught us a moral lesson about freedom and responsibility.[138]

Yuli Tamir, Apr 7, 2024

What has taken place over the last 200 days in Gaza is the most transparent genocide in all of human history. It is the first time that the daily atrocities were broadcast and seen by the peoples of the world in real time. Past genocides have been known almost totally in retrospect through official reports, films and memoirs, which reconstruct horrifying events but after a passage of time. [...] It is a tragic, dehumanizing ordeal, above all for children. It is further shocking that Israel should remain insulated from denunciation and accountability despite its continuing practice of such extreme criminality.[139]

Richard Falk, May 3, 2024

Israel was defeated and is still being defeated, not because of the fact that at the start of the ninth month of this accursed war, Hamas has not been toppled.
    The emblem of defeat will forever appear alongside the menorah and flag, because the leaders, commanders and soldiers of Israel killed and wounded thousands of Palestinian civilians, sowing unprecedented ruin and desolation in the Gaza Strip. [...]
    The defeat, forever, lies in the fact that a state that views itself as the heir of the victims of genocide carried out by Nazi Germany has generated this hell in less than nine months, with an end not yet in sight. [...]
    [T]he majority of Israeli Jews let the drive for revenge blind them. The unwillingness to listen and to know, in order to avoid making mistakes, is in the DNA of the debacle.
    Our all-knowing commanders did not listen to the female spotters, but they mainly failed to listen to Palestinians, who over decades warned that the situation cannot continue like this.[140]

Amira Hass, Jun 4, 2024

I, Lee Mordechai, a historian by profession and an Israeli citizen, bear witness in this document to the horrible current situation in Gaza as events are unfolding. The enormous amount of evidence I have seen, [...] has been enough for me to believe that Israel is currently committing genocide against the Palestinian population in Gaza. I explain why I chose to use the term below. The current war is ostensibly the Israeli reaction to the Hamas massacre of Oct. 7, 2023, a war crime and crime against humanity that was committed within the context of the longstanding conflict between Israelis and Palestinians that can be dated back to 1917 or 1948 (or other dates). In all cases, I do not believe that historical grievances and atrocities justify additional atrocities in the present. Therefore, I consider Israel's response to Hamas' actions on Oct. 7 utterly disproportionate and criminal. [...] I write this publicly to testify that during the war there were and remain Israeli voices who strongly dissented from Israel's actions.[141]

Lee Mordechai, June 18, 2024

I once asked myself if there was anything that Israel could do, bar killing all Palestine's first-born, that would lead the US to cut off the arms supply and declare the experiment with a 'Jewish' State at an end. Today I'm not even sure that killing the first born would suffice. [...]

Today it is clear that there are no limits. If Israel announced gas chambers for the Palestinians Biden would probably query the type of gas and say that this was a red line. When Israel began the killing his red line would disappear into the mists just as happened with the invasion of Rafah.[142]

Tony Greenstein, October 14, 2024

'No daylight between the United States and Israel' is a phrase that has recently joined 'special relationship' and 'unbreakable bond' in the lexicon of US-Israel relations. The metaphor of 'no daylight' implies that the two nations' interests are so closely knit together that nothing and no one can come between them. To see daylight between the two countries would suggest separation and betrayal. But 'no daylight' also means darkness, a fitting metaphor for the blindness that has characterized the special relationship between the United States and Israel. We must let in daylight if Americans are to understand why and how this bond has come to be seen as unbreakable.[143]

Amy Kaplan, 2018

Millions of Jews in America feel connected to Israel's creation. Maybe our ancestors gave or raised money, maybe they went and fought, maybe they donated to Zionist organizations. What's a Jew to do now? Everyone makes their own choices, but my experience of war crimes taught me that being Jewish means standing against any nation that commits war crimes. Any. [...]

An eye for an eye—or a hundred eyes for one eye—is not a thing in international law. A key tenet of the laws of warfare is that an attack that endangers civilians must be militarily necessary and any civilian casualties that occur must be proportional to the military gain. What that means, in plainer language, is that you cannot slaughter a lot of civilians for a minor battlefield gain, and you certainly cannot target civilians, as appears to have happened in the killing of Hala Khreis and many other Palestinians. So far, more than 30,000 people have been reported killed in Gaza, most of them civilians, including more than 13,000 children.

The victims of genocide—which Jews were in the Holocaust—are not gifted with the right to perpetrate one. [...]

This puts all Americans, not just American Jews, on the spot. The US government is Israel's principal supporter, by virtue of the bombs and other weapons that continue to be provided to the extremist government of Prime Minister Benjamin Netanyahu. We are all implicated.[144]

    Peter Maass, April 9, 2024

Clearly what is happening in Gaza today is unspeakable, but what makes it even more painful is that much of this has been done with US weapons and American taxpayer dollars. In the last year alone, the US has provided $18 billion in military aid to Israel and delivered more than 50,000 tons of military equipment.

In other words, the United States is complicit in these atrocities. That complicity must end. [...] It is time to tell the Netanyahu government that they cannot use US taxpayer dollars and American weapons in violation of US and international law and our moral values.[145]

    US Senator Bernie Sanders, November 19, 2024

III.3 Unbending the Arc: Genocide, Complicity, and Responsibility

The US establishment insists that Israel is a healthy democracy and it is capable of moving towards a two state solution in which Palestinians live side by side with Israelis.

No expert on the situation believes as much; but these fictions sustain our political class. [...]

Seeing Israel for what it really is would expose the failure of Zionism. Its principal goal was to create Jewish safety. But Jews are unsafe in Israel because the society is oppressing an indigenous people, which resists. As my mother's best friend assured me in Jerusalem 18 years ago, 'There will be one war after another till they accept us.'

There are always pragmatic rationalizations for denial. If there is no illusion of a two-state solution to wave at people, then the most powerful country in the Middle East will be destabilized, and there will be a bloody and unending rollercoaster (as someone once put it) toward equal rights for all.

But we are plainly in such a savage reality now, and the US establishment is siding with Jewish supremacists. And Palestinians are paying the terrible price for dishonesty and self-righteousness. Don't say you didn't know.[146]

Phillip Weiss, July 15, 2024

I know how painful it is for Jews to grasp that a Jewish state could possibly commit a genocide. But speaking with moral clarity about what is happening to Palestinians at this moment is the only thing 'Never Again' means, if it is to mean anything at all.[147]

Stefanie Fox, 2024

III.4 Critical Distinctions: Antisemitism, Zionism, and Judaism

Zionism was founded on the certainty that antisemitism is inescapable and that we can only mitigate, but can never destroy, it. But today, it's clearer than ever that the Zionist project has failed in its supposed mission to ensure Jewish safety.[148]

Shane Burley and Ben Lorber, 2024

[T]here was a Zionist slogan, 'a land without a people for a people without a land,' intimating that Palestine was an empty land. But the Zionists knew right from the beginning that there was no land without a people. And both Vladimir Jabotinsky and Ben-Gurion, in almost identical words, said that when the Arabs fight against us, it's not terrorism, it's nationalism; they're fighting for their own land, just as we would in their situation. So, they were clear about this. Then you get the horrors of the Second World War, and the worst and the most horrific imaginable expression of events of antisemitism and racism in history. And now you have the identification of the Jewish state with Jewish survival and the fight against antisemitism. So that when a lot of the Eastern European Jews who emigrated to Palestine then came up against the Arabs, the local Arabs who, for perfectly valid reasons as Ben-Gurion and Jabotinsky pointed out, opposed the takeover of their land, they just saw them as another bunch of antisemites. So [...] there's been this confusion right from the beginning.[149]

Gabor Maté, November 6, 2019

If you told me to boil down [...] what is Judaism about [...] I would tell you tikkun olam. It means [...] the repair of the world. I don't want to be part of a Judaism that is being used, taken in my name, to kill and occupy and imprison millions of Palestinians.[150]

Rabbi Ari Lev Fornari, October 28, 2023

Though no one can know how the current ferment within American Judaism will evolve, it seems clear that Zionism is in retreat. Its advocates will have to come to grips with the manner in which it distorted history and created a story of the creation of the State of Israel and its treatment of Palestine's indigenous population which bears no relation to reality. For Judaism, it is becoming increasingly clear, Zionism was a dangerous wrong turn.[151]

Allan C. Brownfeld, June 5, 2023

We need a basic analysis of power and history to understand that Hamas' attacks on Israeli civilians, while egregious, had nothing to do with those Israelis' religion and everything to do with occupation and settler colonialism. [...]

Jews can grieve for Israeli lives lost and refuse the weaponization of that grief to commit genocide against Palestinians. [...]

You are not being an ally to Jews when you quietly watch Israel decimate Gaza. A future in which the world has watched Israel commit genocide against millions of Palestinians in the name of Jews everywhere is not a safer future for my Jewish children.

Israel's policies have never been about Jewish safety. Does it make Jews safer to uproot Palestinians' olive trees? Does it make Jewish Israelis safer to pay them to move to West Bank settlements to replace Palestinians? Does it make Jews safer to render Gaza uninhabitable? Of course not. These policies are consistent with a desire to remove Palestinians from their land—the same motivation behind Israel's current carpet bombing and invasion of Gaza.[152]

Anna Baltzer, November 12, 2023

The Jewish God I studied, the Jewish values I was made to memorize, are manipulated into Land grabbing madness and the impunity to kill. Unless the Jewish God got completely overturned to a Zionist one there should be values shared here, I want us to restudy the Torah together.

And in the meantime I will criticize their sponsored, indoctrinated fate, and there is nothing antisemitic about that. Religious Jewish people settling on Palestinian Land are operating with impunity and protection as an extension of the Israeli arm of domination and ethnic cleansing. There is nothing antisemitic about criticizing that. There is nothing antisemitic about criticizing Israel. There is nothing antisemitic about a Palestinian flag. Let's leave this binary thinking so we can see the crystalline differentiation between being Jewish and using Judaism as a disguise for Israel's agendas of power and greed.[153]

meital yaniv

The definition that was ostensibly formulated to defend Jews across the globe from forms of racial governance, not only ends up legitimizing and shielding a form of racial governance that is presented as democracy, but also becomes a weapon used to strike down pro-Palestinian activism. In this sense, it is a counterinsurgency tool. [...]

One might say that the definition has transformed into a Golem of sorts, a mystical giant and powerful creature created from clay by a famous Rabbi to defend Jews from manifestations of antisemitism. And like the Golem who over time became extremely violent, destructive, and uncontrollable, the IHRA definition of antisemitism has become [unwieldy], and is now being used as a shield not to protect Jews, but to enable Israel to exert genocidal violence against the Palestinians and attack those who dare criticize the violence. Eventually, the Rabbi who made the Golem was forced to destroy his creation, understanding that the Golem had become dangerous to the very community it was created to protect.[154]

Neve Gordon, March 22, 2024

'Let your memory teach you empathy and your suffering teach you love' writes Rabbi Shai Held ('Passover's Radical Message Is More Vital Than Ever,' April 21, 2024) in his Passover message. What we Jews need today, however, is not, as Rabbi Held puts it, a 'revolution in empathy' for Palestinians, but a revolution in how we think about the State of Israel. What we need—urgently—is to come to the recognition that our ethnic nationalist project has been an understandable but catastrophically misguided answer to our history of suffering. Held's invocation of the biblical injunction to 'love the stranger that resides with you' rankles in particular. The Palestinians are not the 'stranger,' but a people whom we have robbed of their homeland in our pursuit of self-determination and safety. Our story this Passover is not about what has been done to us but about what we are doing to another. Held captive to an ideology of conquest and dispossession, it is we Jews who have tragically become capable of the bestiality visited on us over the millennia. Until this is the story we can tell, the future is grim not only for the Palestinians but for the Jews of Israel, who, like the Palestinians of Gaza and the West Bank, and the hundreds of thousands of Palestinian refugees still longing for return, deserve a future of dignity and safety in a shared land.[155]

Mark Braverman, April 2024

'If you protest against the genocide, and then a lot of people come out and say, that's offensive to Jewish people, people will associate Jewish people with committing a genocide, and that makes us infinitely less safe. Jewish people aren't committing a genocide. Israel is and Israel does not represent all of the Jewish people. And by using the Jewish people to shield Israel from any criticism will lead to an unbelievable amount of antisemitism.'[156]

Jared, a Jewish student at Columbia who did not want his last name used because his family was threatened after he publicly supported the Palestinian cause, May 3, 2024

There is nothing remotely antisemitic in holding a nation-state—including the Jewish nation-state—accountable for egregious abuses and violations of human rights. There is nothing antisemitic in standing against a genocide happening in real time. There is nothing antisemitic in protesting US complicity in that genocide. And there is nothing antisemitic in protesting Jewish organizations standing on the wrong side of justice.

For this Jew, I consider it my obligation in every part of my being to join with Palestinians and others across the world who are saying no to the unconscionable destruction of Palestinian society and no to the enormous brutality against the Palestinian people of Gaza.[157]

Donna Nevel, May 11, 2024

In our opinion, to use the memory of the Holocaust like this to justify either genocide in Gaza or repression on college campuses is a complete insult to the memory of the Holocaust.

The dehumanization of Palestinians, describing them as 'human animals,' the killing of tens of thousands of civilians, indiscriminate bombing, the destruction of universities and hospitals, and the use of mass starvation—these are clearly stages of ethnic cleansing and genocide. They cannot be defended any more than sending weapons to commit this genocide or refusing funding to UNRWA. With no better arguments, our politicians have resorted to misusing the memory of the Holocaust while claiming that protesting against Israeli genocide is somehow antisemitic.

As Holocaust survivors, we have no special authority on the Middle East but we do know about antisemitism. It's simply wrong to claim that it's antisemitic to oppose Israeli genocide. It's also wrong to claim that calling for equal rights for Jews and Arabs 'from the river to the sea' is antisemitic.

As Holocaust survivors, we are just a few individuals, but we want to add our voices to the growing global movement to demand a permanent ceasefire, an Israeli withdrawal from Gaza, and for the West to stop arming and supporting genocide.[158]

Ten Holocaust Survivors, June 22, 2024

It's just astonishing to hear people say 'Stop War' is somehow antisemitic. On a very basic level, as a Rabbi my spiritual tradition demands that we pursue peace and that we pursue Justice. The claim that this is antisemitic is absurd on its face. It shows the desperation of those who stand with Israel unconditionally. It shows the patent immorality of that position. [...]

There is a strong constituency that is demanding a fair, humane, and just foreign policy and an end to this genocide. People often say this is just focusing on one issue. In a time of genocide, genocide is the only issue.[159]

Rabbi Brant Rosen, August 18, 2024

III.5 Praying With Our Feet: Jewish Values in Action

'Thou shalt not stand idly by the blood of thy neighbor' (Leviticus 19:15). This is not a recommendation but an imperative, a supreme commandment.[160]

Abraham Joshua Heschel, 1996

The 2 main constituencies organizing for Gaza right now are Palestinians whose family members are under the bombs, and progressive American Jews, many of whom lost family in the Hamas attack. This is an incredible coalition that should give everyone courage. No excuse, speak up.[161]

Rebecca Pierce, Oct 18, 2023

[W]e need to go again and again because we cannot let these tactics of intimidation stop us from standing in solidarity with Palestinians.[162]

Sydney Levy, October 24, 2024

By rabbis being public, it allows for lay people who feel isolated in their congregations or isolated where they are because the people in the front of the room are supporting this war, allows them to see that there are people of moral authority, people connected to the tradition, who are opposed to this war and fighting for a ceasefire. So we also have a very symbolic role that gives other people the ability/permission to advocate for a ceasefire wherever they are, and not feel so, so isolated. In the last two months, [...] the most emotional or a [...] challenging moment for me was in Philadelphia, some Palestinians had a demonstration that was a prayer service outside of Senator Casey's office out in the streets. And there were a few hundred people and there were a group of 60 or 80 Muslims who held the evening prayer service and memorial service out in public for the people who were killed. And they asked some rabbis to come. Part of their memorial service was they read the names of 100 children who were killed in Gaza. And they asked me to say the Jewish prayer for the dead, [...] they asked me after the names were read to say Kaddish. I was in front of a group of Muslims at our prayer service standing next to somebody holding a Palestinian flag. And I was saying Kaddish for children who were murdered by the Israeli army. It was hard. It was hard.[163]

Rabbi Mordechai Liebling, May 14, 2024

On July 23, 400 members of Jewish Voice for Peace peacefully occupied the United States Capitol to demand that the United States stop funding the Israeli military as it destroys life and land in Gaza. I was surrounded by my community, hundreds of Jewish Americans who are resolutely committed to the freedom and safety of Palestinians. We reject the way the Israeli government has manipulated our sacred tradition to justify the mass murder of Palestinians.

In the midst of the protest, I had the honor of leading my fellow protesters in the Shema, the most sacred prayer in Judaism, which reminds us that all of us are *echad*, all are one. When I recite the Shema, I am reminded that Jewish safety is intertwined with Palestinian safety, that no one is free until all of us are free. I called out to my community: 'When we say the Shema, we are declaring that all people are one. Today, we say it to declare that we are here, because we are one with the Palestinian people.' I called the words and 400 others joined me. As a rabbi and as a Jew, I have recited this prayer countless times, but I will never forget this moment where I felt not only our collective grief, but also our collective commitment to fighting for a world of safety and freedom for all.

As I finished praying the final word, with the sound of the Shema still echoing in the rotunda, a police officer grabbed my arms and handcuffed me, adding my name to the tens of thousands of others this past year, including thousands of American Jews, who were arrested for calling on the United States government to end the Israeli military's destruction of Gaza. [...]

As a Jew, I understand how the crime of genocide reverberates for generations. As a rabbi, I am also horrified by the way the Israeli government is exploiting our sacred tradition to justify its brutal campaigns.

On this holy day, we reflect on our transgressions. We admit to our complicity in doing wrong and causing harm. We choose not to turn away from all that needs to be changed. And we commit to *tikkun olam*, the repairing of the world. In our name—our Jewish name—the United States continues to send billions of dollars to the Israeli military government. This is an utter betrayal of Jewish values.

The Jewish tradition teaches that pikuach nefesh, saving a soul, is the single most important obligation of every human being. The Israeli military, funded by the US government, is destroying whole lives each and every day. So on the holiest week of the year, Jewish tradition inspires me to demand that our government stop sending weapons to the Israeli military.[164]

Rabbi Linda Holtzman, October 7, 2024

On Friday, April 26, a delegation from Rabbis for Ceasefire from the US joined Israeli rabbis and Jews in a public attempt to deliver food aid to the people of Gaza through the Erez border crossing. As we marched toward the crossing with bags of rice and flour, we chanted the words of the Passover Haggadah: *Kol dichfin yeitei v'yeichol*—let all who are hungry come and eat.

While food aid is essential, it is not sufficient. To save the lives of Palestinians on the verge of death by Israel's policy of forced starvation and siege, there must be significant infrastructure in place to supply and distribute food, with medical advice and supervision. This is not possible without a cease-fire and lifting the siege.

Unlike the right-wing settlers blocking aid from entering, we were immediately stopped, and myself and six others were arrested. The rest of the group retreated and brought the aid we had sought to bring to the starving people of Gaza to the West Bank, where Palestinians are the targets of vigilante settler violence, land theft, and military intimidation.

I was held for nearly 10 hours at the Ashkelon police station. The Israeli police officer who interrogated me after my arrest said, 'You are being detained because you tried to bring bags of rice and flour into Gaza.' Ultimately, we were released after agreeing to stay away from the Gaza border for 15 days.

Our success was not, of course, from bringing food into Gaza. The Israeli police prevented that. Rather, our nonviolent action succeeded in shining a light on Palestinians on the verge of death by starvation, offering them our solidarity, and reminding Jews of our responsibility to live our lives in accordance with the most sacred value of our beautiful tradition: We are each made in the image of the divine.[165]

Rabbi Alissa Wise, May 9, 2024

The false idol of Zionism has been allowed to grow unchecked for far too long. So tonight we say it ends here. Our Judaism cannot be contained by an ethnostate, for our Judaism is internationalist by its very nature. Our Judaism cannot be protected by the rampaging military of that ethnostate, for all that military does is sow sorrow and reap hatred, including hatred against us as Jews. Our Judaism is not threatened by people raising their voices in solidarity with Palestine across lines of race, ethnicity, physical ability, gender identity and generations. Our Judaism is one of those voices and knows that in this chorus lies both our safety and our collective liberation. [...]

[L]ook around. This here is our Judaism. As waters rise and forests burn and nothing is certain, we pray at the altar of solidarity and mutual aid, no matter the cost. We don't need or want the false idol of Zionism. We want freedom from the project that commits genocide in our name. We want freedom from the ideology that has no plan for peace, except for deals with the murderous, theocratic petrostates next door, while selling the technologies of robo-assassinations to the world. We seek to liberate Judaism from an ethnostate that wants Jews to be perennially afraid, that wants our children afraid, that wants us to believe that the world is against us so that we go running to its fortress, or at least keep sending the weapons and the donations flowing.[166]

Naomi Klein, April 24, 2024

[At a Jewish-led action in Washington, DC in which 300 were arrested] I want to say that rabbis must be calling for a ceasefire right now, no matter what their politics are. [...] We cannot be silent when genocide happens to another people, we have to say, not in our name. [...] We were singing and chanting. We were praying.[167]

Rabbi May Ye, December 8, 2023

ILANA: I remember seeing rabbis outside of Congress. You know, I am a person who's deeply involved in Jewish life, and I have been called directly an antisemite. And so for me, seeing rabbis wrapped in talitot and holding Torah and calling for a humane solution and end to violence. For me, it was just, it was just so powerful to be able to feel like my Judaism is my own.

MIRIAM: Amen. Amen. [...] I remember looking around and thinking, my God, these are some of the greatest rabbinic minds that I've ever had the privilege to learn with and to pray with. [...] And I just kept thinking, I can't believe all these people are alive at the same time. And then thinking that they're all alive at the same time and they're all called to stop this right now.

I have a colleague, Rabbi Salem Pierce, she reminded us that Rabbi Abraham Joshua Heschel went to DC during the Vietnam War because he said, 'I can't open my siddur, I can't open my prayer book to pray without seeing napalm bombs on children. When I open the siddur, I see napalm bombs dropped on children.' And she said, 'That's why I've come to DC. Because I can't open my siddur and not see bombs falling on Gaza.' And we did pray. We did open our siddurs. But to say, we're gonna open our siddurs and we're gonna not deny what's happening, we're gonna publicly with all our might and all our force, in our davening name what is happening and demand that it stop. And demand that it stop happening in our name and with our tax dollars as American Jews, in addition to as rabbis.[168]

Ilana Levinson and Rabbi Miriam Grossman, February 13, 2024

III.6 A Moral Reckoning: Statements of Conscience

For the world is in a bad state, but everything will become still worse unless each of us does his best. So let us be alert—alert in a twofold sense: Since Auschwitz we know what man is capable of. And since Hiroshima we know what is at stake.[169]

Viktor E. Frankl, 1984

People of conscience must reject apartheid in Israel just as clearly and forcefully as we reject white supremacy in the United States. This is not just a political issue for us; it is a moral/spiritual issue. [...] It is a commitment to the foundational principle of Judaism, that every human being is of infinite value, deserving of dignity, freedom, equality and justice.[170]

Rabbi Brian Walt, February 17, 2021

It is no small task to challenge the state of Israel and its practices, even for an Israeli citizen like myself. However, doing so is not only imperative, but is in line with a major trajectory within Jewish history and culture committed to social justice.[171]

Jesse Benjamin, October 12, 2010

My name is Sofia Orr, and I refuse to enlist in the Israeli army because there are no winners in war. Only losers. Everyone living here is losing. [...]

When I was 16, I visited the West Bank with my classmates on a school trip. We talked with settlers and Palestinian boys our age. When we spoke with the Palestinian youth, one of my classmates asked what was their dream in life. And one of them answered, 'The only dream a person locked in a cage can have is to get out.' That sentence has stayed with me and is now the reason I refuse to enlist: I will not take part in a system that is the problem, and not the solution. A system that damages security instead of maintaining it. I refuse to enlist in order to show that change is needed and that change is possible. I refuse to enlist for the security and safety of all of us in Israel-Palestine, and in the name of empathy that is not restricted by national identity.

I refuse to enlist because I want to create a reality in which all children between the river and the sea can dream without cages.[172]

Sofia Orr, March 4, 2024

Before I refused to serve and spent 110 days in prison, people tried to convince me to join the army so I could be the 'nice soldier' at the checkpoints. They believed I could make a difference in how Palestinians were treated and many served in the army for that reason. As if the oppression, occupation or massacre can be moral if the soldiers were more moral. The truth is, there is no moral form of oppression. It is not about individual soldiers or units in the West Bank or Gaza and how they treat the Palestinians, it is the fact that there are soldiers there in the first place. The whole Israeli military is responsible for systematic oppression, occupation, massacre in Gaza and ethnic cleansing.[173]

Mattan Helman, May 5, 2024

My name is Yuval and I live in Jerusalem. For the past 6 years I served as a combat medic paratrooper in the Israeli army. First as conscript and later as a reservist. I am also one of 42 reservists who published an open letter of refusal following Israel's invasion of Rafah in May. [...]

At the war's outset, I was serving [as a medic] in some of the Israeli towns that were destroyed during the attack. We witnessed houses burned down, cars punctured from bullets, destruction everywhere. Nearly everyone I know, including myself, lost someone that was close to them, most of which were unarmed civilians. Those traumatic events have brought Israeli public opinion to the darkest point I've ever seen. [...]

The level of destruction I saw in Gaza was beyond all imagination. [...] Our daily lives in Gaza were carried out in people's homes, where I felt the absence of the Palestinian families who were forced to flee, and I was left sitting among their belongings. We used those homes to protect ourselves from Hamas's snipers, but tactical decisions ended up mixing with soldiers' sentiment of revenge: the homes we stayed in were vandalized, graffiti was done, and small souvenirs were taken from each home. When my commanding officer ordered us to burn down the house we stayed at, justifying his orders with military reasons not nearly legitimate enough to take away the home of a few families, I declared that I'm not willing to participate and left.

The day-to-day reality I witnessed on the ground, as time went on, with the hostages still in captivity reminded me that when given the option, Israel is only willing to resort to military force. [...]

My experiences in Gaza [...] have all led me to believe that militarism is only a source of pain, for both Palestinians and Israelis. [...]

In the name of nonviolence, I also believe that war refusal offers hope. Not only to end the assault on Gaza, but to also rehabilitate communities in the 'Gaza envelope' by breaking the endless cycle of suffering.[174]

Yuval Green, August 5, 2024

All our choices were made to reflect and confront us in the present—not to say, 'Look what they did then,' rather, 'Look what we do now.' Our film shows where dehumanization leads, at its worst. It shaped all of our past and present. Right now we stand here as men who refute their Jewishness and the Holocaust being hijacked by an occupation, which has led to conflict for so many innocent people. Whether the victims of October the 7th in Israel or the ongoing attack on Gaza, all the victims of this dehumanization, how do we resist?[175]

Jonathan Glazer, March 10, 2024

We are proud Jews who denounce the weaponization of Jewish identity and the memory of the Holocaust to justify what many experts in international law, including leading Holocaust scholars, have identified as a 'genocide in the making.' We reject the false choice between Jewish safety and Palestinian freedom. We honor the memory of the Holocaust by saying: Never again for anyone. [...]

We were alarmed to see some of our colleagues in the industry mischaracterize and denounce his remarks [...] Their attacks on Glazer are a dangerous distraction from Israel's escalating military campaign which has already killed over 32,000 Palestinians in Gaza and brought hundreds of thousands to the brink of starvation. We grieve for all those who have been killed in Palestine and Israel over too many decades, including the 1,200 Israelis killed in the Oct. 7 Hamas attacks and the 253 hostages taken. [...]

We should be able to name Israel's apartheid and occupation—both recognized by leading human rights organizations as such—without being accused of rewriting history.[176]

Joaquin & Rain Phoenix, Joel Coen, Tom Stoppard, Ilana Glazer, et al, April 6, 2024

I can no longer in good conscience represent this administration amidst President Biden's disastrous, continued support for Israel's genocide in Gaza. [...]

What I have learned from my Jewish tradition is that every life is precious. That we are obligated to stand up for those facing violence and oppression, and to question authority in the face of injustice. [...]

The United States has long enabled Israeli war crimes and the status quo of apartheid and occupation. That status quo does not keep Israelis safe, nor Jews around the world. It certainly does not protect Palestinians, who have the right to freedom, safety, self-determination, and dignity, just as much as Jewish people do, and every person does. Any system that requires the subjugation of one group over another is not only unjust, but unsafe. Jewish safety cannot—and will not—come at the expense of Palestinian freedom. Making Jews the face of the American war machine makes us less safe. [...]

I urge you all to take a stand for Palestinian lives. All of our futures depend on this.[177]

Lily Greenberg Call, May 15, 2024

I recently entered an Israeli consulate and submitted papers to formally renounce my citizenship. [...]

In its genocidal campaign to erase Palestine's Indigenous people, the state has weaponized my very existence, my birth and identity—and those of so many others. The wall that keeps Palestinians from returning home is constituted as much by identity papers as by concrete slabs. Our job must be to remove those concrete slabs, to rip up the phony papers, and to disrupt the narratives that make these structures of oppression and injustice appear legitimate or, god forbid, inevitable. [...]

As a traditional Jew, I believe the Torah is radical in its contention that Jewish people, or any people, have no *right* at all to any land, but rather are bound by rigorous ethical responsibilities. [...]

The struggle for a liberated Palestine is linked to the struggle of Indigenous Land Back movements everywhere.

My single citizenship is but one brick in [the] wall. Nevertheless, it is a brick. And it must be physically removed.[178]

Avi Steinberg, December 26, 2024

III.7 The College Campus: Dissent, Repression, and Resistance

> *Those Jews who identify conscience and justice as central to Judaism and Jewish life have every right, indeed a moral obligation, to speak on behalf of Palestinians, and therefore, on behalf of what they see as the essence of Judaism. The attempt to censor this speech and the speech of others on college campuses—college campuses playing a historically vigorous role in promoting free and open debate—as anti-Semitic is wrong and should be opposed.*[179]
>
> Marc Ellis, 2004

As of today, it has been a month since the Oct. 7 attacks that have dominated global political consciousness and discourse, not to mention our experiences as young Jewish people. Zionist institutions purport to be representative of all Jews, often using us as a rhetorical shield to support the unconscionable actions of the state of Israel. We feel a particular pain as Jews having to continuously justify our stance against genocide. We are here to make ourselves clear: We stand in solidarity with Brown Students for Justice in Palestine and the Palestine Solidarity Caucus in the pursuit of the liberation of Palestinian peoples. We know intimately that Jewish struggles are necessarily bound up in global struggles for freedom. We are a group of Jewish students who have coalesced around our shared vision of justice, anti-occupation, liberation and community. We ask you to listen to us now. [...]

We will not shy away from calling out injustice in the world; we will not let our Jewish identity be co-opted. Our Judaism compels us to oppose the Israeli state. [...]

We write these words from the diaspora, and it is from here that we wish to better our world. As we grapple with millennia of Jewish struggle and survival, we will not abandon our Palestinian cousins and peers or let them stand alone. This genocide cannot continue.

Not in our names. With or without our names: *Never*.[180]

A collective of anti-occupation Jews, November 7, 2023

Yale Jews for Ceasefire exists because of—not in spite of—our Jewish values. On the issue of divestment, for example, the Talmud teaches us that we may not sell weapons to those we suspect of using them criminally. Therefore, we have a duty to disrupt the manufacture and sale of military weapons that kill others, including those killing Palestinians. [...]

On Passover of all holidays, Jews are compelled to feel the suffering of oppressed people. We eat bitter herbs to remind ourselves of the bitterness of slavery in Egypt, and we dip parsley in salt water to symbolize the tears of our ancestors. The story of oppression is all too familiar to the Jewish people—and it is our duty to combat oppression in all its forms, for Jews and non-Jews alike.

We also teach the story of Nachshon, who took the first brave steps into the stormy Red Sea as the Jewish people fled Egypt. He did not know what would happen, but he had faith that he would make it to the other side. By stepping up in a precarious moment, he became a leader of his people, convincing them to follow in his footsteps—literally—into the unknown.

Our present moment is a precarious one for the Jewish people, fraught with disagreement about what our Jewish values mean to us. But Nachshon teaches us that when we have the courage to lead, we can encourage others to move forward with us, toward a world free of oppression and violence. At Yale, organizers of all faiths continue to build a community that is dedicated to moving forward in collaboration with, not opposition to, Jewish students.[181]

Ian Berlin, April 27, 2024

What happened with the president of Harvard and Penn and all of these right wing people all of a sudden becoming defenders of Jews against antisemitism is such crass manipulation. [...] In this next year, where we're going to be involved in very intense organizing to protect our democracy to protect our rights, let's not fall into the trap of [villainizing] the other. [...] [L]et's also show true solidarity with each other.[182]

Rabbi Mordechai Liebling, May 14, 2024

I've been listening to some of the interviews with Jewish students who feel threatened. And often it appears to me […] that many of them feel threatened because they see a Palestinian flag, because they hear people calling for intifada. 'Intifada' means 'shaking off.' There's a very similar word in Hebrew for it, *'lehitna'er.'* It's what a dog does when it shakes off water. It's to shake off the occupation. And there are Jewish students, often who are influenced by their Israeli friends, who feel that that is threatening.

But there's nothing threatening about opposing occupation and oppression. That is not antisemitism. You can agree with it or not. Even being anti-Zionist is not antisemitic. There are hundreds of thousands, if not more, of ultra-Orthodox Jews, including some who are in the Israeli government, who are anti-Zionist, but they're not antisemitic. They see themselves as the epitome of Jewishness and Jewish tradition. So, there's politics, and there's prejudice. And if we don't make a distinction between the two, then what we are actually doing is enforcing a kind of silence over the policies that have been conducted by the Israeli government for a long time and that ultimately culminated now in the utter destruction of Gaza.[183]

Omer Bartov, April 30, 2024

The most important thing is to focus on the limits on expression, which are pretty far out on the horizon. Free expression, free inquiry, academic freedom all have to be given broad range for protection. Where there's actual threatening behavior, that can be restricted. That can be precluded. […] But provoking people, challenging people, asking difficult questions, making people uncomfortable, that's part of the price of living in a democracy, if you will. That's what it means to live in a self-governing society. […]

We have been far too loose with what we mean by threatened, and not just in the past few months, but in the past few years. Many people feel that when they hear views that they deeply disagree with, that's threatening to them. That's not how universities operate. You are not entitled to be intellectually safe. You are entitled to be physically safe.[184]

Frederick Lawrence, May 2, 2024

As I worked with students and administrators at schools across the country—helping them to parse vital distinctions between criticism of Israel and antisemitism, disagreement and bigotry, discomfort and danger—I came to appreciate the necessity of considering each campus conflict in all its particularity. Some incidents were simple, others complex. But in each case, I found that the way to understand the situation was to carefully examine it, rather than rush to judge it. In a moment when many American Jews are feeling afraid, in a media environment that is stoking that fear with headlines that conflate many different kinds of events, it is more important than ever to proceed with level-headed calm. To undertake this sorting and disaggregation of a vertiginous pile of anecdotes will help us not only to more accurately assess the threat to Jews on campuses, but also to guard against Jewish fear being used to erode civil liberties.[185]

Ben Lorber, November 28, 2023

If I can be fired for criticizing a foreign government, calling attention to a genocide and using my academic expertise as an anthropologist to draw attention to how power operates, then no one is safe, I wasn't fired for anything I said in the classroom. I was fired because of a charge brought by a student I had never met, let alone taught, who had been surveying my social media account for months. This isn't about student safety, this is about silencing dissent. We are witnessing a new McCarthyism and we should all be terrified of its implications.[186]

Dr. Maura Finkelstein, September 27, 2024

As Jewish academics, researchers, and higher education professionals, we are appalled by, and refuse to accept, the deliberate mischaracterization, and weaponization of persisting fears about Jewish safety and well-being on campuses across the United States as the singular excuse for a series of misguided and dangerous policies by university administrators. [...]

We call on our fellow Jewish academics and the Jewish community at large to recognize that this remarkable movement to stop a genocide being committed in our name has emerged not from some dangerous alien source but from our own children, siblings, parents, and friends. This movement – our movement – represents a living recommitment to social and international justice by our community and many others. [...]

We invite people of all faiths and heritages to join the Palestine solidarity movement in the full commitment for freedom and equality for everyone between the river and the sea—and indeed, between every river and every sea as the world enters an ever more perilous era.[187]

Jewish Voice for Peace Academic Advisory Council, May 13, 2024

We're witnessing something that I'm not sure I ever thought we would witness, which is that the struggle for Palestinian liberation has really captured the minds of kind of a whole generation of young Americans—and very quickly—and is convulsing America's universities in a way that no foreign policy issue has in at least a generation. ...This movement holds the possibility in a way that no movement in America has in my entire lifetime to end American institutional complicity with the oppression of the Palestinian people...We must see the lie that you can construct a system of Jewish safety on the destruction and brutalization of another people. [...]

[S]ystems of violence ultimately endanger everybody. [...] [T]he only way [Israelis] can be truly safe is if Palestinians are truly safe. And the only way that Palestinians can be truly safe is if Palestinians are free. [...]

And so, when we see this movement and what's happening, it offers, it seems to me, the kernel of us being able to imagine a different future: a future of mutual respect, and mutual equality, and mutual safety, and mutual liberation. And we desperately, perhaps above all else in this moment of harm, we need that sense of hope.[188]

Peter Beinart, April 28, 2024

III.8 Affirming the Prophetic: Hope in Action

And if we do act, in however small a way, we don't have to wait for some grand utopian future. The future is an infinite succession of presents, and to live now as we think human beings should live, in defiance of all that is bad around us, is itself a marvelous victory.[189]

Howard Zinn, 2002

How do we keep going? How do we keep going for Gaza? How do we keep going for mutual safety for all Palestinians and Israelis? How do we keep going for all of us here? How do we keep the flame of our shared humanity alive? We act. We act and we do not wait for hope. We act and our actions draw hope closer back to us.[190]

Rabbi Miriam Grossman, December 7, 2023

On the surface, we might think that hope is about the future. But it exists in that instant between the present and the future. It exists in our heart-mind when we think something good can happen, or that we can, through effort, make it happen. [...] Cultivating hope is a collective call to action. We must not close our hearts if we want to engage hope. [...] The pain becomes the fuel for action.

Ground in gratitude, face and feel the grief over what is, form a vision of what could be and set forth together to realize that vision. That is the practice of Active Hope [as defined by Joanna Macy].[191]

Rabbi Meryl Crean, Kol Nidre 5785/2024

What will it take to build a world where this nightmare is unthinkable, where every single life is precious, where all children run safely into their parent's arms at the end of a school day?

It is unbearable to not have the answers. But I do know this: the only thing greater than our horror, more profound than our heartbreak, bigger than our overwhelm at the task at hand must be our determination to answer the questions through action.[192]

Stefanie Fox, May 23, 2024

A permanent ceasefire in Gaza is an urgent matter that all Jews should be supporting.

The call for Ceasefire Now that has been building around the world is predicated on the assumption that there is no military solution, and there has never been. […]

Neither Palestinians nor Israelis can be safe unless Palestinians have justice. Peace with justice is the only possible road to the humanistic vision of sharing the land in a society premised on equality. The call for a permanent ceasefire is not simply a slogan; it is a plan of action, a plan for peace, and a plea to end the systematic destruction of an entire society.[193]

Rebecca Alpert, December 28, 2023

[I]f there appears little short-term prospect of peace taking root in Gaza's scorched soil, seeds of hope have sprouted elsewhere, as a solidarity movement of unprecedented size and vigor sprang to Gaza's defense. In Western Europe and North America, massive demonstrations have mobilized for week after week opposing Israel's onslaught. Progressive Jews are in the militant vanguard. In the United States and Britain, public opinion backs an immediate cease-fire in Gaza, even as not one major political party endorsed this position. […] [H]undreds of officials have risked their careers to demand an end to complicity in Israel's war crimes. Gaza has become a symbol for injustice, inequality, and the hypocrisies of power writ large, and around this symbol, the glimmer of a New International can be espied.[194]

Jamie Stern-Weiner, December 29, 2023

If we let go of Zionism, Israel—the country, or even better, the land itself—may have the chance of truly becoming a just and equitable polity of all its citizens, and the Jewish diaspora may flourish without Israel as its necessary center. In a more prophetic register, the Jews themselves may have the chance to move that much closer to what we've so often aspired to be: *a light unto the nations*.[195]

Shaul Magid, 2023

A Jewish theology of liberation confronts Holocaust and empowerment with the dynamic of solidarity, providing a bridge to others as it critiques our own abuses of power.[196]

Marc Ellis, 2004

I'm hopeful. I'm not optimistic. I am hopeful. I see a difference. I think optimists are people who believe that it will be okay but there's nothing we can do about it. They are optimistic by nature. I'm hopeful, and by that I mean that there are discrete processes that at this moment in time may seem destructive, but I think have the potential to work for liberation of Palestine and the end of apartheid Israel and replacement by a democratic state. [...] I don't think we should observe these processes. [...] I think we should be part of them.[197]

Ilan Pappé, July 31, 2024

And years from now, when the history of this genocide is written, we will be asked: Did we speak out? And if so, what did we say? What did we risk?

For now, that book is still open, even if every new page is becoming increasingly unbearable to read. Even if the world would rather move on to another story.

We all have a part to play in bringing this genocide to an end soon, in our own day. How will we write ourselves into this book when it is finally recorded?

May we all play our part in bringing this book of the genocide to a finish. May it come to an end soon, in our own day. And when it does, may we come to understand it was only part of a larger story—an even greater book that will conclude with these glorious words: 'Then Palestine was finally free, from the river to the sea.'[198]

Brant Rosen, October 3, 2024

Aftermath of the bombardment by an Israeli airstrike on Khan Yunis, Gaza Strip, 20 March 2025. Photo by: Doaa Albaz. Activestills Photo Collective, all rights reserved.

Acknowledgements

My gratitude list is composed of people who provided indispensable support, kindness, and generosity, to me and for this project, either at critical stages or throughout the process.

Two beloved longtime friends, Rebekah Rosenfeld and Anna Beresin, are the midwives for this project. Each contacted me after 7 October 2023 with the suggestion that it was time for a third booklet using the format of the 2008 and 2013 *Thou Shalt Not Stand Idly By* booklets. As a published author, Anna shared resources and boundless encouragement. When technology was daunting and dispiriting, Anna recommended I contact her son, Gabe Beresin. Now a young adult, Gabe had been my first-grade student during the years I taught in our congregational Sunday school. He was delighted to provide the spirit and skills that allowed me to continue to write.

Alison Glick, an author, activist, and dear friend, and her husband Jim Strick, a seasoned academic and author, took interest in this project; each offered time, providing specific support to keep things moving. George Graves has been a steadfast comrade, backing me with assistance needed in support of the editing process.

Hannah Mermelstein's editorial genius, consummate knowledge of the material, kindness, and patience brought this project to fruition. As an experienced Palestine solidarity activist and librarian, Hannah shepherded me with respect and grace through the final stages of this project.

A best friend is essential in an undertaking that gives one's heart and soul a regular workout. Thank you, Katherine Kurtz, for your unflappable commitment to the importance of this project, and confidence in me.

Over many years, my niece, Jaime Gordon, has lovingly supported my work for justice in Palestine with interest and open mind. At the eleventh hour, she offered technical assistance needed to cross the finish line.

Three additional people complete this list: my college professor Howard Zinn set me on an early course to recognize, understand, and address systemic injustice on a national and global scale. Rabbi Brian Walt first introduced me to Palestinians as the indigenous people who have legitimate historic claims, connection, and love for the land that is Israel. In 2009 Mark Braverman fortuitously named and shaped what became a significant focus for my work by underscoring the role of Jews in supporting Christian churches to take the lead in mobilizing a movement for justice in Palestine, as they bravely had done during the Civil Rights Movement and the anti-Apartheid movement in South Africa. Kairos theology and interfaith alliances continue to inspire and guide me, as does my ongoing collaboration and friendship with Mark.

Finally, to the centuries of Jews of conscience who have guided me, whose voices I have shared in this book, my gratitude is infinite and eternal.

Voices

Rebecca Alpert is a Reconstructionist Rabbi and professor emerita of Religion at Temple University.

Arielle Angel is the editor-in-chief of *Jewish Currents Magazine*.

Hannah Arendt (1906–1975) was a German-born philosopher who fled to France after Hitler's rise to power in 1933 and then immigrated to the United States in 1941. She supported a Zionism based in a renewed Jewish presence in Palestine, but opposed a Jewish state.

Uri Avnery (1923–2018) fled from Germany to France and then Palestine to escape Hitler. As a teen he was a member of the Zionist terrorist organization, Irgun. He founded Gush Shalom, the Israeli Peace Bloc, in 1973, and was a prolific Israeli peace activist committed to a just peace.

Anna Baltzer is an author, public speaker, and activist for Palestinian human rights.

Omer Bartov is an Israeli-American historian of the Holocaust and Genocide Studies. He teaches at Brown University and has published books and edited volumes on these topics.

Elisha Baskin is an Israeli who has been a member of Boycott from Within and served on the Board of Jewish Voice for Peace.

Elliott batTzedek is a poet, liturgist, and bookseller in Philadelphia. She is a co-founder and co-leader of Fringes: a feminist, non-zionist havurah.

Dov Baum lived in Israel most of her adult life and became an anti-occupation activist while working and living in Israel. She is a feminist activist and scholar, and the director of corporate accountability and research for the American Friends Service Committee.

Peter Beinart is a journalist and political commentator for *Jewish Currents, The New York Times, MSNBC, The Atlantic*, and more. He is the author of many books, including the 2025 title *Being Jewish After the Destruction of Gaza: A Reckoning*.

Joel Beinin is professor emeritus of History and Middle East Studies at Stanford University. He has written and edited books on topics such as labor movements, social movements, and Israel/Palestine.

Shlomo Ben-Ami is a former Israeli diplomat, politician, and historian. He is a co-founder and Vice President of the Toledo International Center for Peace, and professor emeritus at Tel Aviv University.

Jesse Benjamin is a sociologist and anthropologist whose research has focused on racial theory, coloniality, Pan-African theory, and Israel/Palestine.

Phyllis Bennis is an American Jewish writer, activist, and political commentator. She is a strong critic of Israel and the United States, and a leading advocate for Palestinian rights.

Rabbi Elmer Berger (1908–1996) was a Reform rabbi and Executive Director of American Council on Judaism (ACJ), an organization formed in 1942 to combat the Reform movement's embrace of Zionism. He was an advocate of the universal prophetic and classical Reform traditions in Judaism, and an outspoken opponent of Jewish nationalism and Zionism.

Ian Berlin graduated from Yale University in 2024. He is a journalist and has participated in and published on protests against the war on Gaza.

Natan Blanc is an Israeli conscientious objector who has served numerous prison terms for his refusal to serve in the Israeli military.

Max Blumenthal is a journalist, author, blogger, and filmmaker.

Mark Braverman is a psychologist, author, and fifth-generation Palestinian Jew who grew up in the United States. He is the Executive Director of Kairos USA.

Eitan Bronstein Aparicio is an Israeli educator and co-founder of De-Colonizer, a research and art laboratory. He was also founder and director of the Israeli NGO Zochrot, which works to promote awareness of the Palestinian Nakba among Jewish Israelis.

Allan C. Brownfeld is a syndicated columnist, associate editor of the *Lincoln Review,* and editor of *Issues*, the quarterly journal of the American Council for Judaism. He is a contributing editor to the *Washington Report on Middle East Affairs*.

Martin Buber (1878–1965) was a philosopher, theologian, and proponent of cultural Zionism. He was born in Vienna and immigrated to Palestine in 1938, where he taught at Hebrew University and advocated for a binational state founded on Arab-Jewish equality.

Avraham Burg is an Israeli politician, author, and businessman who served in leadership roles in the Israeli Knesset, the Jewish Agency, and the World Zionist Organization before coming to criticize political Zionism and calling for an end to Israel's apartheid regime.

Shane Burley is a journalist and filmmaker based in Portland, Oregon. He is the co-author of *Safety through Solidarity: A Radical Guide to Fighting Antisemitism*.

Judith Butler is an American feminist philosopher, gender studies scholar, and author. They are a Distinguished Professor in the Graduate School at University of California, Berkeley.

Lily Greenberg Call is a political activist and former public servant. On May 15, 2024, she became the first Jewish presidential appointee to resign over President Biden's support for Israel's genocide in Gaza.

Noam Chomsky is professor emeritus at the Massachusetts Institute of Technology. He is a linguist, analytic philosopher, activist, and author of over 100 books, including the 1983 title *The Fateful Triangle: The United States, Israel and the Palestinians*, which has been updated and re-released multiple times since its publication.

Joel Coen is an Academy Award-winning filmmaker. He was among hundreds of Jewish creatives to sign a letter in support of Jonathan Glazer's Oscar Speech in April 2024.

Rabbi Meryl Crean is a Reconstructionist rabbi who has worked for peace with justice in Israel/Palestine. She is active in interfaith work with Christian-Jewish Allies and is a member of the Rabbinical Council of Jewish Voice for Peace.

Ben Ehrenreich is an American novelist and freelance journalist whose essays and criticisms appear in mainstream and alternative press. He is the author of several books, including *The Way to the Spring: Life and Death in Palestine*.

Albert Einstein (1879–1955) was a German-born mathematician and physicist who developed the theory of relativity. While he supported Jewish settlement in Palestine, he opposed the creation of an independent Jewish state.

Marc Ellis (1952–2024) was a professor, Jewish liberation theologian, and author and editor of more than twenty books on Jewish Studies. He argued that the Jewish prophetic tradition was at odds with Zionism.

Hedy Epstein (1924–2016) was a Holocaust survivor and political activist who worked with the International Solidarity Movement and others in her support for Palestinian rights.

Richard Falk is professor emeritus of international law at Princeton University. He has authored dozens of books and served as the United Nations Special Rapporteur about human rights in the Palestinian territories.

Maura Finkelstein is a writer, professor, and cultural anthropologist who was fired from her tenured position at Muhlenberg College in 2024 for pro-Palestinian speech.

Norman G. Finkelstein is an American political scientist and activist who has done extensive research and writing about the Holocaust and about Israel and Palestine.

Simha Flapan (1911–1987) was an Israeli politician, activist, and one of Israel's well-known "New Historians." His book *The Birth of Israel: Myths and Realities* was published the year he died.

Rabbi Ari Lev Fornari is a White, queer, trans person of Ashkenazi and Italian descent, and is the senior rabbi at Kol Tzedek synagogue in Philadelphia.

Stefanie Fox, an organizer and strategist with a commitment to Palestinian liberation and a Jewish future beyond Zionism, is the Executive Director of Jewish Voice for Peace.

Viktor Frankl (1905–1997) was an Austrian neurologist, psychologist, philosopher, and Holocaust survivor. He was the author of *Man's Search for Meaning*.

Sigmund Freud (1856–1939) was an Austrian neurologist and the founder of psychoanalysis. He is often called the "father of modern psychology."

Chavka Fulman-Raban (1924–2014) was one of the last survivors of the Warsaw Ghetto Uprising and a fierce critic of the Israeli occupation of Palestine.

Masha Gessen is a Russian American journalist, author, and translator who has written prolifically about politics and LGBTQ rights.

Joseph F. Getzoff is a cultural geographer and professor of International Studies at Boston College. He has researched and written on settler colonialism and neoliberal Zionism.

Ilana Glazer is an American actor, director, producer, comedian, and activist. She was among hundreds of Jewish creatives to sign a letter in support of Jonathan Glazer's Oscar Speech in April 2024.

Jonathan Glazer is an English Jewish film director and screenwriter who won an Academy Award for *The Zone of Interest*, a Holocaust drama. In his 2024 acceptance speech, he denounced Israel's war on Gaza.

Alison Glick is a teacher, administrator, author, and activist. She has lived in the West Bank, Gaza, and Yarmouk refugee camp, and maintains strong connections with friends and family in Gaza.

Rabbi Shai Gluskin is the former education director of the Jewish Reconstructionist Federation. He sits on the Rabbinical Council of Jewish Voice for Peace.

Nahum Goldman (1894–1982) was President of the World Zionist Organization from 1956-68, and President of the World Jewish Congress. He spoke out in favor of negotiations with the PLO in the mid-1980s.

Neve Gordon is an Israeli professor of human rights and international law at Queen Mary University in London.

Rabbi Lynn Gottlieb is one of the first 10 women rabbis in modern Judaism. She organizes for racial, indigenous, and gender justice and Palestinian liberation. She is a founding member of the Rabbinical Council of Jewish Voice for Peace.

Yuval Green served as a medic in the Israeli reserves at the start of Israel's war on Gaza, and refused to continue in 2024.

Tony Greenstein is a British anti-Zionist and a founding member of the Palestine Solidarity Campaign. Greenstein is also a trade unionist, author, blogger, and son of a rabbi.

David Grossman is an Israeli novelist and long-time peace activist.

Rabbi Miriam Grossman is a Jewish educator, ritual maker, writer, and organizer. She is co-chair of Tirdof: New York Jewish Clergy for Justice.

Ahad Ha'am (1856–1927) was born Asher Ginzberg in Russia. Known as the founder of cultural Zionism, he adopted the pseudonym Ahad Ha'am ("A man of the people"). He supported a Hebrew renaissance but was opposed to political Zionism from the beginning of Zionist settlement in Palestine.

Jeremiah (Jerry) Haber is the nom de plume of Charles Manekin, professor emeritus of philosophy and Jewish Studies at the University of Maryland. He is the creator of the blog "The Magnes Zionist: Self-criticism from an Israeli, American, and Orthodox Jewish Perspective."

Jeff Halper is an American-Israeli anthropologist and activist. He is the founder and director of the Israeli Committee Against House Demolitions and a co-founder of the One Democratic State Campaign.

Amira Hass is the daughter of two Holocaust survivors and the only Israeli journalist who lives full-time among Palestinians, in Gaza from 1993 and in Ramallah since 1997. She writes mostly about the West Bank and Gaza for the Israeli newspaper *Haaretz*.

Mattan Helman is the Executive Director of Refuser Solidarity Network (RSN) and has been imprisoned several times for his refusal to serve in the Israeli army.

Rabbi Abraham Joshua Heschel (1907–1972) was a Polish-American rabbi, important Jewish theologian, and leader in the Civil Rights Movement.

Rabbi Linda Holtzman, ordained in 1979, is a Reconstructionist rabbi in Philadelphia. She is the leader of the Tikkun Olam Chavurah, a community dedicated to social justice locally and in Israel-Palestine. Rabbi Linda is a member of the Jewish Voice for Peace Rabbinical Council and Rabbis for Ceasefire.

Adam Horowitz is Managing Editor for Mondoweiss, an independent news website that focuses on reporting about Israel/Palestine.

Bella Jacobs is a 2024 graduate from Pitzer College, where she was active in Jewish Voice for Peace and Students for Justice in Palestine.

Tony Judt (1948–2010) was an English historian, essayist, and professor of European Studies at New York University. An avid Zionist as a teenager, he began to question the movement after the 1967 war, and began to advocate for one binational state in 2003.

Amy Kaplan (1953–2020) was the Edward W. Kane Professor of English at the University of Pennsylvania and president of the American Studies Association in 2003–2004. She is the author of *Our American Israel: The Story of an Entangled Alliance*.

Naomi Klein is a Canadian author and social activist known for her political analyses and criticism of corporate globalization. She has been active in the Boycott, Divestment, and Sanctions movement (BDS) and made sure the Hebrew translation of her book The Shock Doctrine was done in a way that aligned with BDS guidelines.

Irena Klepfisz is a lesbian poet, activist, and retired Barnard College professor. She and her mother survived the Warsaw Ghetto, though her father was killed in the Warsaw Ghetto Uprising. She co-founded the Jewish Women's Committee to End the Occupation of the West Bank and Gaza.

Brian Klug is an Honorary Fellow in Social Philosophy at Campion Hall, Oxford and an emeritus member of the philosophy faculty at Oxford University. He is a co-author of the *Jerusalem Declaration on Antisemitism*, a response to the *IHRA Definition of Antisemitism*.

Joel Kovel (1936–2018) was an American scholar, psychiatrist, author, and human rights activist. His book *Overcoming Zionism: Creating a Single Democratic State in Israel/Palestine* was published in 2007.

Yitzhak Laor is an Israeli poet, author, and journalist. His book *The Myths of Liberal Zionism* was published in 2009.

Frederick Lawrence is an American lawyer and civil rights scholar, and is the former president of Brandeis University.

Shamai Leibowitz is an Israeli-American human rights lawyer. He is an Orthodox Jew and part of a group of Israeli soldiers who has refused to serve in the Occupied Territories. He is the son of Yeshayahu Leibowitz.

Yeshayahu Leibowitz (1903–1994) arrived in Jerusalem in 1945 from Latvia and became a scientist at Hebrew University and a writer on Judaism, ethics, and politics. As a humanist, he was described as the "conscience of Israel."

Joseph Levine is a philosopher and professor emeritus at the University of Massachusetts, Amherst. He has been active in groups working for Palestinian rights since 1982.

Ilana Levinson is an audio journalist and founder of the Unsettled, a podcast about Israel-Palestine and the Jewish Diaspora.

Gideon Levy is an Israeli journalist for the *Haaretz* newspaper, where he writes opinion pieces and a weekly column that often focus on Israel's occupation of Palestine.

Sydney Levy is the former advocacy director for Jewish Voice for Peace, and has recently volunteered in the West Bank with the Center for Jewish Nonviolence. He is a member of JVP's BIJOCSM (Black, Indigenous, Jews of Color, Sephardi and/or Mizrahi) network.

Rabbi Mordecai Liebling is the Senior Advisor for POWER Interfaith, the largest faith-based community organizing group in Pennsylvania. He has held leadership roles at the Social Justice Organizing Program at the Reconstructionist Rabbinical College, Jewish Funds for Justice, the Shefa Fund, and the Jewish Reconstructionist Federation.

Rabbi Ellen Lippmann is the founder and rabbi emerita of Kolot Chayeinu/Voices of Our Lives congregation in Brooklyn, NY. She is a former co-chair of the board of T'ruah.

Ben Lorber is a senior research analyst at the social justice think tank Political Research Associates, researching antisemitism and white nationalism. He is the co-author of *Safety through Solidarity: A Radical Guide to Fighting Antisemitism*.

Ian Lustick is a professor of Political Science at the University of Pennsylvania. He specializes in modern Middle East politics and has written widely on Israel/Palestine and the US war on terror.

Peter Maass is an American journalist and author who has written for *The Wall Street Journal, The New York Times*, and *The Washington Post*.

Shaul Magid is a rabbi and a professor of Jewish Studies at Harvard Divinity School and Dartmouth College.

Rabbi Judah Magnes (1877–1948) was born in San Francisco and moved to Palestine in 1922. He was the first president of Hebrew University, a pacifist, and an advocate for a binational state.

Gabor Maté left Hungary for Canada with his Holocaust-survivor parents in 1956, and later spent more than a decade working as an addictions specialist on Vancouver's Downtown Eastside. In recent years, Maté's groundbreaking work linking trauma and disease has risen to global prominence.

Rela Mazali is an Israeli feminist writer, lecturer, and peace activist who co-founded the New Profile movement to challenge militarism and support conscientious objectors.

Edwin Samuel Montagu (1879–1924) was a British Liberal politician and the third practicing Jew to serve in the British cabinet. He opposed the Balfour Declaration and political Zionism.

Lee Mordechai is a Byzantine environmental historian and Israeli citizen.

Marilyn Kleinberg Neimark is a co-founder of Jews for Racial and Economic Justice and has been active in the Palestine/Israel peace movement since the 1980s. She has been a co-host of Beyond the Pale on WBAI Radio in New York and is a professor emerita at Baruch College–The City University of New York.

Donna Nevel is a community psychologist and long-time Jewish activist and organizer for Israeli-Palestinian peace and justice. She is co-director of PARCEO, which has created a curriculum on antisemitism from a framework of collective liberation.

Sophia Orr is an Israeli teenager who spent 85 days in military prison in 2024 for refusing to enlist in the Israeli army.

Amos Oz (1939–2018) was an Israeli-born writer, novelist, and journalist as well as a professor of literature at Ben Gurion University. He advocated a two-state solution to the Israel-Palestine conflict.

Ilan Pappé is an Israeli historian, political scientist, and former politician. He left Israel in 2008 after being condemned by the Knesset, and now works in Social Sciences, International Studies, Palestine Studies, and Ethno-Political Studies at the University of Exeter in the UK. His most recent book is *Lobbying for Zionism on Both Sides of the Atlantic*.

Miko Peled is an Israeli American activist, international speaker, and karate instructor. He is the author of *The General's Son: The Journey of an Israeli in Palestine*.

Rebecca Pierce is a Black Jewish filmmaker and writer based in San Francisco. She has created documentary films, podcasts, political essays, and sketch comedy.

Yoram Peri is a sociologist and media scholar, professor emeritus of Israel Studies at the University of Maryland, and former political advisor to the late Israeli Prime Minister Yitzhak Rabin. He was editor-in-chief of the Israeli newspaper *Davar* and a board member of the New Israel Fund.

Joaquin & Rain Phoenix are brother and sister, both actors. Joaquin has won several Academy Awards for his distinguished performances. The two were among hundreds of Jewish creatives to sign a letter in support of Jonathan Glazer's Oscar Speech in April 2024.

Tanya Reinhart (1943–2007) was professor emerita of Linguistics and Comprehensive Literature at Tel Aviv University. She had a regular column in *Yediot Aharonot*, the largest circulation Israeli daily newspaper, and was known for her poignant critique of Israel's policy toward the Palestinian people.

Adrienne Rich (1929–2012) was an American poet, essayist, feminist, and supporter of Black, queer, and Palestinian liberation struggles.

Rabbi Brant Rosen is the founder of the first anti-Zionist Jewish Reconstructionist congregation in Evanston, IL. He has been active in Jewish Voice for Peace's Rabbinical Council, and is the author of *Wrestling in the Daylight: A Rabbi's Path to Palestinian Solidarity*.

Alice Rothchild is a retired OB-GYN and current author and activist for Palestinian rights. She has worked with the Health and Human Rights Project, written fiction and nonfiction books about Israel/Palestine, and co-produced *Voices Across the Divide*, a documentary and oral history project.

Sara Roy is an economist and scholar in Middle Eastern Studies at Harvard University. She has spent time in and written about the economy of Gaza.

Senator Bernie Sanders is an American politician and activist who is the senior United States senator from Vermont. He is a staunch outspoken advocate for income equality and universal healthcare for all, and a critic of Israeli policy.

Heike Schotten is a professor in Political Science and Women's, Gender, and Sexuality Studies at the University of Massachusetts Boston.

Sarah Schulman is an American author, activist, and AIDS Historian. She is a Distinguished Professor of the Humanities at College of Staten Island (CSI), and has organized an LGBTQ delegation to Palestine, a tour of queer Palestinian leaders in the US, and the Homonationalism and Pinkwashing conference at the City University of New York.

Hannah Schwarzschild is a Philadelphia-based attorney and Palestine solidarity activist. She is a cofounder of Fringes: a feminist non-zionist havurah. She is the daughter of Henry Schwarzschild.

Henry Schwarzschild (1925–1996) was born in Berlin and arrived in the US in 1939, shortly after his bar mitzvah. He was a civil rights activist and opponent of the death penalty. His 1982 public statement repudiating Zionism was prompted by the horrors of Israeli actions in the first Lebanon war.

Raz Segal is an Israeli historian living in the US. He is a professor of Holocaust and Genocide Studies at Stockton University and a leading authority on genocide.

Yonatan Shapira is an ex-captain and pilot in the Israeli Air Force, and authored a 2003 letter signed by 27 pilots explaining their refusal to serve in the Occupied Palestinian Territories. He is an activist who has been part of the Freedom Flotilla intended to break the siege of Gaza.

Avi Steinberg is an Israeli-born author and essayist who has explored the intersections between the books we read and the lives we live.

Jamie Stern-Weiner is a doctoral student at University of Oxford researching the politics of antisemitism. He is the editor of *Moment of Truth: Tackling Israel-Palestine's Toughest Questions*.

I.F. Stone (1907–1989) was born to a Russian Jewish family in Philadelphia and became one of the giants of the Left in the United States. He was a journalist, editor, and author.

Tom Stoppard is a Czech-born British playwright and screenwriter whose work highlights human rights and political freedom. He was among hundreds of Jewish creatives to sign a letter in support of Jonathan Glazer's Oscar Speech in April 2024.

Yuli Tamir is an Israeli academic and former politician. She is the President of Beit Berl Academic College and was one of the founders of Peace Now.

Nathan Thrall is an American writer based in Jerusalem, a professor at Bard College, and author of the Pulitzer Prize-winning book *A Day in the Life of Abed Salama: Anatomy of a Jerusalem Tragedy*.

Rebecca Vilkomerson is the co-directory of Funding Freedom, organizing with philanthropy to better support Palestinian liberation. She was the Executive Director of Jewish Voice for Peace from 2009 to 2019.

Rabbi Brian Walt is founder and rabbi emeritus of the Reconstructionist synagogue Mishkan Shalom, and former Executive Director of Rabbis for Human Rights, North America. He was born in South Africa and shaped by the politics of the movement against Apartheid, and he blogs, writes, and speaks about justice in Israel-Palestine.

Phillip Weiss is a journalist, founder, and co-editor of Mondoweiss: The War of Ideas in the Middle East, a progressive website that covers American foreign policy news about Israel/Palestine.

Rabbi Alissa Wise is the lead organizer for Rabbis for Ceasefire and co-author of *Solidarity is the Political Version of Love: Lessons from Jewish Anti-Zionist Organizing*. She co-founded the Jewish Voice for Peace Rabbinical Council and was a staff leader at JVP from 2011 to 2021.

meital yaniv is a queer, trans, Israeli-born artist, writer, filmmaker, and anti-Zionist Jew.

Rabbi May Ye is a Chinese-American Jew from unceded Wabanaki land. She creates ritual and liturgy to uplift those who have been marginalized in Jewish communities, and is an activist committed to Palestinian liberation.

Oren Yiftachel is an Israeli professor of political and legal geography and urban planning at Ben Gurion University. He has worked with the Israeli human rights organization B'tselem and is an author of many books, including *Ethnocracy: Land and Identity Politics in Israel/Palestine.*

Dorothy M. Zellner is the daughter of non-Zionist secular Jewish immigrant parents, and a long-time activist for civil rights and social justice. She was active in Freedom Summer and the Student Nonviolent Coordinating Committee (SNCC). She is a founding member of Jews Say No!, has volunteered with Physicians for Human Rights, and is an active supporter of the Boycott, Divestment, and Sanctions movement (BDS).

Rabbi Laurie Zimmerman is the rabbi at the Reconstructionist synagogue Shaarei Shamayim. She writes and teaches frequently about Israel/Palestine and is the author of a curriculum called *Reframing Israel: Teaching Kids to Think Critically About Israel.*

Howard Zinn (1922–2010) was an American historian, playwright, philosopher, socialist intellectual, and World War II veteran. He was a professor at Spelman College and Boston University, and authored more than twenty books, including the influential *A People's History of the United States.*

Zochrot is an Israeli NGO that exposes and disseminates information about the Palestinian Nakba in Hebrew, promotes accountability among the Jewish public of Israel, and works toward the implementation of the right of return for Palestinian refugees.

Notes

I. Reclaiming Jewish Voices of Conscience on Israel-Palestine, Spring 2008

1 Marc H. Ellis, *Israel and Palestine—Out of the Ashes: The Search For Jewish Identity in the Twenty-First Century* (Pluto Press, 2002), p. 178.

2 *Nationalism and the Jewish Ethic: Basic Writings of Ahad Ha'am*, ed. by Hans Kohn (Schocken Books, 1962), pp. 122–23.

3 Ro Oranim, 'What Did Freud Really Think of Zionism?', *The Librarians*, 8 September 2019, https://blog.nli.org.il/en/freud_on_zionism/

4 *Prophets Outcast: A Century of Dissident Jewish Writing about Zionism and Israel*, ed. by Adam Shatz (Nation Books, 2004), p. 206.

5 Martin Buber and Paul R. Mendes-Flohr, *A Land of Two Peoples: Martin Buber on Jews and Arabs* (Oxford University Press, 1983), pp. 321–22.

6 Simha Flapan, *The Birth of Israel: Myths and Realities* (Pantheon, 1987), p. 8.

7 Jeff Halper, *Obstacles to Peace: A Reframing of the Palestinian—Israeli Conflict*, 4th edn (Palestine Mapping Center, 2005).

8 Edwin Montagu, 'Memorandum of Edwin Montagu on the Anti-Semitism of the Present (British) Government—Peace with Justice, Security and Equal Rights for Israelis and Palestinians', 22 October 2012, https://britainpalestineproject.org/edwin-montagu-and-zionism-1917/

9 Martin Buber and Paul R. Mendes-Flohr, *A Land of Two Peoples: Martin Buber on Jews and Arabs* (Oxford University Press, 1983), p. 61.

10 Arthur A. Goren, *Dissenter in Zion: From the Writings of Judah L. Magnes* (Harvard University Press, 1982), p. 62.

11 *Prophets Outcast: A Century of Dissident Jewish Writing about Zionism and Israel*, ed. by Adam Shatz (Nation Books, 2004), pp. 62–64.

12 Arthur A. Goren, *Dissenter in Zion: From the Writings of Judah L. Magnes* (Harvard University Press, 1982), p. 46.

13 Jack Ross, *Rabbi Outcast: Elmer Berger and American Jewish Anti-Zionism* (Potomac Books, 2011), p. 63.

14 Martin Buber and Paul R. Mendes-Flohr, *A Land of Two Peoples: Martin Buber on Jews and Arabs* (Oxford University Press, 1983), pp. 183–84.

15 Hannah Arendt, *The Jew as Pariah*, (Grove Press, 1978), p. 181.

16 *Prophets Outcast: A Century of Dissident Jewish Writing about Zionism and Israel*, ed. by Adam Shatz (Nation Books, 2004), p. 251.

17 Sara Roy, 'Living with the Holocaust: The Journey of a Child of Holocaust Survivors', *Institute for Palestine Studies*, 32.1 (2002), https://www.palestine-studies.org/en/node/41147

18 *Prophets Outcast: A Century of Dissident Jewish Writing about Zionism and Israel*, ed. by Adam Shatz (Nation Books, 2004), p. 397.

19 Gary V. Smith, *Zionism the Dream and the Reality* (Trafalgar Square, 1974), p. 31.

20 Noam Chomsky, *Fateful Triangle: The United States, Israel, and the Palestinians*, revised edn (South End Press, 1999), p. 98.

21 *Wrestling with Zion: Progressive Jewish-American Responses to the Israeli-Palestinian Conflict*, ed. by Tony Kushner and Alisa Solomon (Grove Press, 2003), p. 35.

22 *Wrestling with Zion: Progressive Jewish-American Responses to the Israeli-Palestinian Conflict*, ed. by Tony Kushner and Alisa Solomon (Grove Press, 2003), pp. 176–77.

23 *Prophets Outcast: A Century of Dissident Jewish Writing about Zionism and Israel*, ed. by Adam Shatz (Nation Books, 2004), p. 391.

24 Jerry Haber, 'Zionism without a Jewish State', *The Magnes Zionist*, 12 August 2007, http://www.jeremiahhaber.com/2007/08/zionism-without-jewish-state.html

25 *Prophets Outcast: A Century of Dissident Jewish Writing about Zionism and Israel*, ed. by Adam Shatz (Nation Books, 2004), p. 268.

26 Noam Chomsky, *Fateful Triangle: The United States, Israel, and the Palestinians*, revised edn (South End Press, 1999), pp. 131–32.

27 Sara Roy, 'Living with the Holocaust: The Journey of a Child of Holocaust Survivors', *Institute for Palestine Studies*, 32.1 (2002), https://www.palestine-studies.org/en/node/41147

28 Avraham Burg and International Herald Tribune, 'Opinion | The End of Zionism?: A Failed Israeli Society Is Collapsing', *The New York Times*, 6 September 2003, section Opinion, https://www.nytimes.com/2003/09/06/opinion/IHT-the-end-of-zionism-a-failed-israeli-society-is-collapsing.html

29 Amira Hass, 'It's Not All in the Details—Haaretz Com—Haaretz.Com', *Haaretz*, 29 December 2005, https://www.haaretz.com/2005-12-28/ty-article/its-not-all-in-the-details/0000017f-dc8f-db5a-a57f-dcef37330000

30 Uri Avnery, 'Uri Avnery: Back to the Scene of the Crime | Scoop News', *Gush Shalom*, 12 September 2006, https://www.scoop.co.nz/stories/HL0612/S00256/uri-avnery-back-to-the-scene-of-the-crime.htm

31 Joel Beinin, email to author, 'We Cannot Support the Annapolis Conference', 26 April 2025.

32 Alice Rothchild, 'The Judaization of East Jerusalem', *The Electronic Intifada*, 27 November 2007, https://electronicintifada.net/content/judaization-east-jerusalem/7231

33 Norman G. Finkelstein, *Beyond Chutzpah: On the Misuse of Anti-Semitism and the Abuse of History* (University of California Press, 2005), p. 76.

34 Shamai Leibowitz, 'In Defense of Divestment', *Against the Current*, 114, https://againstthecurrent.org/atc114/p339/

35 Tanya Reinhart, *The Road Map to Nowhere: Israel/Palestine Since 2003* (Verso, 2006), p. 131.

36 Ilan Pappe, 'Palestine 2007: Genocide in Gaza, Ethnic Cleansing in the West Bank', *The Electronic Intifada*, 11 January 2007, https://electronicintifada.net/content/palestine-2007-genocide-gaza-ethnic-cleansing-west-bank/6673

37 Gideon Levy, 'With Friends Like These', *Haaretz.Com*, 23 March 2008, https://www.haaretz.com/2008-03-23/ty-article/with-friends-like-these/0000017f-f4c3-d487-abff-f7ff3f470000
38 Arthur A. Goren, *Dissenter in Zion: From the Writings of Judah L. Magnes* (Harvard University Press, 1982), pp. 277–79.
39 *Prophets Outcast: A Century of Dissident Jewish Writing about Zionism and Israel*, ed. by Adam Shatz (Nation Books, 2004), pp. 62–64.
40 Martin Buber and Paul R. Mendes-Flohr, *A Land of Two Peoples: Martin Buber on Jews and Arabs* (Oxford University Press, 1983), pp. 273–79.
41 Marc H. Ellis, *Israel and Palestine—Out of the Ashes: The Search For Jewish Identity in the Twenty-First Century* (Pluto Press, 2002), pp. 175–78.
42 Grossman, 'A State of Missed Opportunities', *The Guardian*, 7 November 2006, section World news, https://www.theguardian.com/world/2006/nov/07/israel
43 Uri Avnery, 'Facing Mecca', *CounterPunch.Org*, 17 February 2007, https://www.counterpunch.org/2007/02/17/facing-mecca/
44 Phyllis Bennis, *Understanding the Palestinian-Israeli Conflict: A Primer* (Interlink Publishing, 2012), p. 183.

II. Amplifying Jewish Voices of Justice on Israel-Palestine, Winter 2013

45 Ilan Pappe, *The Ethnic Cleansing of Palestine*, 2nd edn (Oneworld Publications, 2007), p. 245.
46 Avraham Burg, *The Holocaust Is Over; We Must Rise From its Ashes* (St. Martin's Press, 2008), p. 237.
47 Jeff Halper, *An Israeli in Palestine: Resisting Dispossession, Redeeming Israel* (Pluto Press, 2008), p. 217.
48 Eitan Bronstein, 'An Israeli on Nakba Day: "Our Humanity Is Bound up with Your Right to Return"', *Mondoweiss*, 16 May 2010, https://mondoweiss.net/2010/05/an-israeli-on-nakba-day-our-humanity-is-bound-up-with-your-right-to-return/
49 Sarah Schulman, 'Opinion | Israel and "Pinkwashing"', *The New York Times*, 23 November 2011, section Opinion, https://www.nytimes.com/2011/11/23/opinion/pinkwashing-and-israels-use-of-gays-as-a-messaging-tool.html
50 Philip Weiss, 'Fear of Democracy in the Jewish Community', *Mondoweiss*, 10 April 2013, https://mondoweiss.net/2013/04/democracy-jewish-community/
51 Judith Butler, 'Judith Butler's Remarks to Brooklyn College on BDS', *The Nation*, 7 February 2013, https://www.thenation.com/article/archive/judith-butlers-remarks-brooklyn-college-bds/
52 Ian Lustick, 'Israel Needs a New Map', *Los Angeles Times*, 21 March 2013, https://www.latimes.com/opinion/la-xpm-2013-mar-21-la-oe-lustick-zionism-obama-israel-20130321-story.html
53 Rabbi Brant Rosen, 'The Village of Iqrit and the Dream of Return', *Shalom Rav*, 10 June 2013, https://rabbibrant.com/2013/06/09/the-village-of-iqrit-and-the-dream-of-return/

54   Elisha Baskin, '10 Takeaways from the Boston University Right of Return Conference', *Mondoweiss*, 15 April 2013, https://mondoweiss.net/2013/04/takeaways-return-conference/

55   Adam Horowitz, 'Knesset Votes down the Two-State Solution', *Mondoweiss*, 8 January 2014, https://mondoweiss.net/2014/01/knesset-votes-solution/

56   Max Blumenthal, *Goliath: Life and Loathing in Greater Israel* (Nation Books, 2013), p. 61.

57   Adrienne Rich, 'Why Support the U.S. Campaign for the Academic and Cultural Boycott of Israel? | MR Online', 8 February 2009, https://mronline.org/2009/02/08/why-support-the-u-s-campaign-for-the-academic-and-cultural-boycott-of-israel/

58   Naomi Klein, 'Transcript of Naomi Klein Lecture in Ramallah', *BDS Movement*, 9 July 2009, https://bdsmovement.net/news/transcript-naomi-klein-lecture-ramallah

59   Anna Baltzer, 'The Privileging of Jewish American Voices on the Issue Is Rooted in Racism', *Mondoweiss*, 8 October 2012, https://mondoweiss.net/2012/10/the-privileging-of-jewish-american-voices-on-the-issue-is-rooted-in-racism/

60   Norman G. Finkelstein, *This Time We Went Too Far: Truth and Consequences of the Gaza Invasion*, revised edn (OR Books, 2010), p. 103.

61   Rela Mazali, 'A Call for Livable Futures', *US Campaign for the Academic and Cultural Boycott of Israel*, 25 June 2010, https://usacbi.org/2010/06/a-call-for-livable-futures/

62   Annie Robbins, 'Rabbi Ellen Lippmann Changes Her Mind on the Boycott', *Mondoweiss*, 15 September 2011, https://mondoweiss.net/2011/09/rabbi-ellen-lippmann-changes-her-mind-on-the-boycott/

63   *The Case for Sanctions Against Israel*, ed. by Audrea Lim (Verso Books, 2012), pp. 189, 191.

64   Rabbi Lynn Gottlieb, 'Where Are We Headed? A Reflection on the 74th Anniversary of Kristallnacht | Freepali.Com', https://www.freepali.com/where-are-we-headed-a-reflection-on-the-74th-anniversary-of-kristallnacht/

65   *The Case for Sanctions Against Israel*, ed. by Audrea Lim (Verso Books, 2012), p. 139.

66   Hedy Epstein, 'Ending Israel's Occupation Is the Only Way to Truly Invest in Palestine', *Mondoweiss*, 30 April 2012, https://mondoweiss.net/2012/04/ending-israels-occupation-is-the-only-way-to-truly-invest-in-palestine/

67   Donna Nevel and Dorothy Zellner, 'Why the BDS Movement Is Effective and Right', *Jewish Currents*, 30 October 2012, https://jewishcurrents.org/why-the-bds-movement-is-effective-and-right

68   Gideon Levy, 'The Israeli Patriot's Final Refuge: Boycott', *Haaretz*, 14 July 2013, section Opinion, https://www.haaretz.com/opinion/2013-07-14/ty-article/.premium/gideon-levy-the-israeli-patriots-final-refuge/0000017f-e0a3-d804-ad7f-f1fb90770000

69   Ira Glunts, 'A Jew, Jesus and Justice for Palestinians: An Interview with Mark Braverman', *Mondoweiss*, 5 June 2013, https://mondoweiss.net/2013/06/palestinians-interview-braverman/

70   Judith Butler, 'Judith Butler's Remarks to Brooklyn College on BDS', *The Nation*, 7 February 2013, https://www.thenation.com/article/archive/judith-butlers-remarks-brooklyn-college-bds/

71   Yitzhak Laor, 'Only by Fear of International Sanctions—Opinion', *Haaretz.Com*, 11 February 2013, https://www.

haaretz.com/opinion/2013-02-11/ty-article/.premium/
yitzhak-laor-only-by-fear-of-sanctions/0000017f-f55e-d5bd-a17f-f77e3d180000

72 Jack Ross, *Rabbi Outcast: Elmer Berger and American Jewish Anti-Zionism* (Potomac Books, 2011), p. 49.
73 Jeff Halper, *An Israeli in Palestine: Resisting Dispossession, Redeeming Israel* (Pluto Press, 2008), pp. 100–02.
74 Howard Zinn, 'The Poisons of Nationalism', *Tikkun*, 1 August 2008, p. 89.
75 Peter Beinart, 'The Failure of the American Jewish Establishment', *The New York Review of Books*, 10 June 2010, https://www.nybooks.com/articles/2010/06/10/failure-american-jewish-establishment/
76 Rabbi Brian Walt, 'Reflections on Liberal Zionism', *Tikkun*, 1 January 2011.
77 Mark Braverman, 'Hostages to Zionism', *Mondoweiss*, 14 February 2011, https://mondoweiss.net/2011/02/hostages-to-zionism/
78 Na'eem Jeenah and others, *Pretending Democracy: Israel, an Ethnocratic State*, ed. by Na'eem Jeenah (Afro-Middle East Centre, 2012), p. 100.
79 Judith Butler, 'Judith Butler's Remarks to Brooklyn College on BDS', *The Nation*, 7 February 2013, https://www.thenation.com/article/archive/judith-butlers-remarks-brooklyn-college-bds/
80 Jerry Haber, 'Who Is a Liberal Zionist?', 11 March 2013, http://www.jeremiahhaber.com/2013/03/who-is-liberal-zionist.html
81 Ian Lustick, 'Israel Needs a New Map', *Los Angeles Times*, 21 March 2013, https://www.latimes.com/opinion/la-xpm-2013-mar-21-la-oe-lustick-zionism-obama-israel-20130321-story.html
82 Shlomo Ben-Ami, 'Israel: The Vision and the Fantasy', *Al Jazeera*, 23 May 2013, https://www.aljazeera.com/opinions/2013/5/23/israel-the-vision-and-the-fantasy
83 *Brant Rosen: Wrestling in the Daylight: A Rabbi's Path to Palestinian Solidarity*, dir. by Todd Boyle (Seattle, 2013), https://www.youtube.com/watch?v=6fw4sLMgrWk
84 Donna Nevel, 'U.S. Jewish Activist: Why I Am Protesting the Friends of the IDF Dinner', *Haaretz.Com*, 7 March 2010, https://www.haaretz.com/2010-03-07/ty-article/u-s-jewish-activist-why-i-am-protesting-the-friends-of-the-idf-dinner/0000017f-e36e-d75c-a7ff-ffef14e30000
85 Yonatan Shapira, 'Journal of a Voyage', *The Only Democracy?*, 26 September 2010, https://theonlydemocracy.org/2010/09/yonatan-shapiras-testimony-from-the-jewish-boat-to-gaza/
86 Hannah Schwarzschild, 'Why They Go: Freedom Riders Then and Now', *The Hill*, 13 May 2011, https://thehill.com/blogs/congress-blog/civil-rights/91260-why-they-go-freedom-riders-then-and-now/
87 Anna Baltzer, 'Message to Presbyterians: "If You Truly Want to Help the Palestinian People, I Urge You to Listen to What They Are Asking For"', *Mondoweiss*, 8 July 2012, https://mondoweiss.net/2012/07/message-to-presbyterians-if-you-truly-want-to-help-the-palestinian-people-i-urge-you-to-listen-to-what-they-are-asking-for/
88 Haggai Matar, 'Young Israeli Conscientious Objector Sentenced to Sixth Consecutive Prison Term', *+972 Magazine*, 13 February 2013, https://www.972mag.com/young-israeli-conscientious-objector-sentenced-to-sixth-consecutive-prison-term/

89 Ben Ehrenreich, 'Is this Where the third Intifada Will Start?', *The New York Times*, 15 March 2013, section Magazine, https://www.nytimes.com/2013/03/17/magazine/is-this-where-the-third-intifada-will-start.html

90 Richard Silverstein, 'Last of Warsaw Ghetto Survivors Calls for Rebellion Against Israeli Occupation', *Tikun Olam*, 10 April 2013, https://www.richardsilverstein.com/2013/04/09/last-of-warsaw-ghetto-survivors-calls-for-rebellion-against-israeli-occupation/

91 Amira Hass, 'The Inner Syntax of Palestinian Stone-Throwing—Opinion', *Haaretz.Com*, 3 April 2013, https://www.haaretz.com/opinion/2013-04-03/ty-article/.premium/amira-hass-the-inner-syntax-of-resistance/0000017f-dbd4-df62-a9ff-dfd7e5c80000

92 Rabbi Brant Rosen, 'Outrage in Gaza: No More Apologies', *Shalom Rav*, 28 December 2008, https://rabbibrant.com/2008/12/28/outrage-in-gaza-no-more-apologies/

93 Ibid.

94 Norman G. Finkelstein, *This Time We Went Too Far: Truth and Consequences of the Gaza Invasion*, revised edn (OR Books, 2010), pp. 103, 140.

95 Rabbi Brian Walt, 'Reflections on Liberal Zionism', *Tikkun*, 1 January 2011.

96 Anna Baltzer, 'The Privileging of Jewish American Voices on the Issue Is Rooted in Racism', *Mondoweiss*, 8 October 2012, https://mondoweiss.net/2012/10/the-privileging-of-jewish-american-voices-on-the-issue-is-rooted-in-racism/

97 Alice Rothchild, 'Lessons from the Civil Rights Movement on an Important Anniversary', *AL.Com*, 16 April 2013, https://www.al.com/opinion/2013/04/lessons_from_the_civil_rights.html

98 Rabbi Brant Rosen, 'A Jew in Solidarity With the Palestinian People', *Shalom Rav*, 29 November 2010, https://rabbibrant.com/2010/11/29/a-jew-in-solidarity-with-the-palestinian-people/

99 Philip Weiss, 'Fear of Democracy in the Jewish Community', *Mondoweiss*, 10 April 2013, https://mondoweiss.net/2013/04/democracy-jewish-community/

100 Marc H. Ellis, 'Exile and the Prophetic: Peter Beinart's "I Love Israel"', *Mondoweiss*, 13 May 2013, https://mondoweiss.net/2013/05/prophetic-beinarts-israel/

101 Philip Weiss, 'Fear of Democracy in the Jewish Community', *Mondoweiss*, 10 April 2013, https://mondoweiss.net/2013/04/democracy-jewish-community/

102 Heike Schotten, 'When "J" Means "Jewish" not "Justice"', *Mondoweiss*, 16 May 2013, https://mondoweiss.net/2013/05/means-jewish-justice/

103 Jeff Halper, *An Israeli in Palestine: Resisting Dispossession, Redeeming Israel* (Pluto Press, 2008), p. 223.

104 Mark Braverman, *Fatal Embrace: Christians, Jews, and the Search for Peace in the Holy Land* (Synergy Books, 2010), p. 188.

105 *The Case for Sanctions Against Israel*, ed. by Audrea Lim (Verso Books, 2012), p. 134.

106 Joel Kovel, '"Zionism's Bad Conscience" (Kovel's First Anti-Zionist Piece, in 2002)', *Mondoweiss*, 30 April 2013, https://mondoweiss.net/2013/04/zionism-conscience-zionist/

107 Joseph Levine, 'On Questioning the Jewish State', *Opinionator*, https://archive.nytimes.com/opinionator.blogs.nytimes.com/2013/03/09/on-questioning-the-jewish-state/

III. Engaging Jewish Voices of Conscience and Dissent

108 Jehad Abusalim, 'It Is neither Death, nor Suicide', *In These Times*, 26 March 2025, https://inthesetimes.com/article/palestine-israel-genocide-resistance-zionism

109 Marc H. Ellis, *Israel and Palestine—Out of the Ashes: The Search For Jewish Identity in the Twenty-First Century* (Pluto Press, 2002), p. 166.

110 Rabbi Brant Rosen, 'Seeking Understanding Amidst the Horror in Israel/Palestine', *Shalom Rav*, 12 October 2023, https://rabbibrant.com/2023/10/12/seeking-understanding-amidst-the-horror-in-israel-palestine/

111 Miko Peled, 'The October Failures', *Mondoweiss*, 7 October 2023, https://mondoweiss.net/2023/10/the-october-failures/

112 Isaac Chotiner, 'Could the Attack on Israel Spell the End of Hamas?', *The New Yorker*, 8 October 2023, https://www.newyorker.com/news/q-and-a/could-the-attack-on-israel-spell-the-end-of-hamas

113 Ilan Pappe, 'My Israeli Friends: This Is Why I Support Palestinians', *Palestine Chronicle*, 10 October 2023, https://www.palestinechronicle.com/my-israeli-friends-this-is-why-i-support-palestinians-ilan-pappe/

114 Arielle Angel, '"We Cannot Cross Until We Carry Each Other"', *Jewish Currents*, 12 October 2023, https://jewishcurrents.org/we-cannot-cross-until-we-carry-each-other

115 Alice Rothchild, 'The Hypocrisy of Israel and "the Most Moral Army in the World"', *Alice Rothchild, MD*, 14 October 2023, https://alicerothchild.substack.com/p/the-hypocrisy-of-israel-and-the-most

116 Rabbi Laurie Zimmerman, 'I Protest this Bloodshed', *Evolve*, 16 October 2023, https://evolve.reconstructingjudaism.org/i-protest-this-bloodshed/

117 Rabbis for Ceasefire, '10/20/23 Statement', *Rabbis for Ceasefire*, 15 February 2024, https://rabbis4ceasefire.com/statements/statement-2/

118 'Zochrot', 30 March 2010, https://olympiarafahmural.org/zochrot-israel

119 Rabbi Shai Gluskin, 'Is it Antisemitic to Consider Zionism a Colonial Project?', *Evolve*, 29 October 2018, https://evolve.reconstructingjudaism.org/isitantisemeticcolonialismzionism/

120 Joseph Getzoff, 'Wasted Lands: Zionist Development and Settler Colonialism in the Naqab/Negev', 2020, p. 32.

121 Jeff Halper, 'Foregrounding the Political and Decolonization after October 7', *Mondoweiss*, 20 October 2023, https://mondoweiss.net/2023/10/foregrounding-the-political-and-decolonization-after-october-7/

122 Norman Finkelstein, 'Nat Turner in Gaza', *Norman Finkelstein*, 26 October 2023, https://www.normanfinkelstein.com/nat-turner-in-gaza/

123 Adam Horowitz, Keynote speech (presented at the IPMN 20th Anniversary Conference, Decatur, Georgia, 22 March 2024).

124 Gideon Levy, 'Just Smile and Call it a Victory. What Matters Is Getting out of Gaza', *Haaretz.Com*, 23 June 2024, https://www.haaretz.com/opinion/2024-06-23/ty-article-opinion/.premium/just-smile-and-call-it-a-victory-what-matters-is-getting-out-of-gaza/00000190-410d-d16c-a7b0-5f8d8ba70000

125 Jamie Stern-Weiner, 'Gaza After the Deluge', *Jacobin*, 29 December 2023, https://jacobin.com/2023/12/gaza-war-israel-occupation-history-war-crimes-hamas-humanitarian-catastrophe

126 Rabbi Brant Rosen, 'Toward a Judaism of Love over Land, People over Profit', *Shalom Rav*, 22 November 2024, https://rabbibrant.com/2024/11/22/toward-a-judaism-of-love-over-land-people-over-profit/

127 *'The Beginning of the End of the Zionist Project'—Ilan Pappé*, dir. by Middle East Eye, 2024, https://www.youtube.com/watch?v=L-YLROxeHA0

128 Abraham Joshua Heschel and Susannah Heschel, *Moral Grandeur and Spiritual Audacity: Essays* (Farrar Straus & Giroux, 1996), p. 231.

129 Sarah Emily Baum, 'Jewish Students Are Bringing their Faith to the Campus Movement for Palestine', *Teen Vogue*, 26 April 2024, https://www.teenvogue.com/story/jewish-students-faith-palestine-university-protests

130 Raz Segal, 'A Textbook Case of Genocide', *Jewish Currents*, 13 October 2023, https://jewishcurrents.org/a-textbook-case-of-genocide

131 Rachel Treisman, 'Despite Backlash, Masha Gessen Says Comparing Gaza to a Nazi-Era Ghetto Is Necessary', *NPR*, 22 December 2023, section Middle East crisis—explained, https://www.npr.org/2023/12/22/1221128897/masha-gessen-essay-israel-gaza-germany-hannah-arendt-prize

132 Mitchell Atencio, 'What Does it Mean to Be an Israeli Against Apartheid?', *Sojourners*, 11 December 2023, https://sojo.net/articles/reconstruct/what-does-it-mean-be-israeli-against-apartheid

133 *Rabbi Gottlieb, Rev. Tanner, Rev. Hammamy and Dr. Michael Spath Discuss the Situation in Gaza*, dir. by Indiana Center for Middle East Peace, 2024, https://www.youtube.com/watch?v=ZHc_s43or3U

134 Alison Glick, 'Of Families, Mills, and Gardens', *Mondoweiss*, 24 February 2024, https://mondoweiss.net/2024/02/of-families-mills-and-gardens/

135 meital yaniv, *Bloodlines* (Communities of Memory, 2023), p. 158.

136 Elliott batTzedek, 'Psalm 137', *Fringes: A Feminist, non-Zionist Havurah*, 15 February 2024, https://fringeshavurah.com/2024/02/15/psalm-137/

137 Gideon Levy, 'When Six Israelis Were Mourned, over 40,000 Palestinians Were Ignored', *Haaretz*, 5 September 2024, section Opinion, https://www.haaretz.com/opinion/2024-09-05/ty-article-opinion/.premium/when-six-israelis-are-mourned-more-than-40-000-palestinians/00000191-be46-dc3b-a7df-ff56b2250000

138 Yuli Tamir, 'We Israelis Are all Complicit in the Starvation of Civilians in Gaza', *Haaretz*, 7 April 2024, section Opinion, https://www.haaretz.com/opinion/2024-04-07/ty-article-opinion/.premium/we-israelis-are-all-complicit-in-the-starvation-of-civilians-in-gaza/0000018e-b476-d906-a5cf-b6f6e1240000

139 Richard Falk, 'Palestine, Iran, and Populist Resistance: The Limits of Law, Morality, and the UN', *Global Justice in the 21st Century*, 3 May 2024, https://richardfalk.org/2024/05/03/palestine-iran-and-populist-resistance-the-limits-of-law-morality-and-the-un/

140 Amira Hass, 'The Destruction, Starvation and Death in Gaza Are Israel's Defeat', *Haaretz*, 4 June 2024, section Opinion, https://www.haaretz.com/opinion/2024-06-04/ty-article/.premium/the-destruction-starvation-and-death-in-gaza-are-israels-defeat/0000018f-e31a-dce5-abdf-e33f1d9a0000

141 Lee Mordechai, 'Bearing Witness to the Israel-Gaza War (Updated to 18 June 2024)', *Academia.Edu*, https://www.academia.edu/112967602/Bearing_Witness_to_the_Israel_Gaza_War_updated_to_18_June_2024_

142 Tony Greenstein, 'Gaza Is Israel's Auschwitz and October 7 Is the Palestinians' Kristallnacht', 14 October 2024, https://tonygreenstein.com/gaza-is-israels-auschwitz-and-october-7-is-the-palestinians-kristallnacht/

143 Amy Kaplan, *Our American Israel: The Story of an Entangled Alliance* (Harvard University Press, 2018), p. 280.

144 Peter Maass, 'Opinion | I'm Jewish, and I've Covered Wars. I Know War Crimes When I See Them', *The Washington Post*, 9 April 2024, https://www.washingtonpost.com/opinions/2024/04/09/israel-gaza-war-crimes-genocide/

145 Bernie Sanders, 'On the Joint Resolutions of Disapproval to Block the Sale of Certain Offensive Arms to Israel', *CounterPunch.Org*, 19 November 2024, https://www.counterpunch.org/2024/11/19/on-the-joint-resolutions-to-block-the-sale-of-certain-offensive-arms-to-israel/

146 Weiss, 'Israel Is Falling Apart, and American Leaders Are in Denial', *Mondoweiss*, 15 July 2024, https://mondoweiss.net/2024/07/israel-is-falling-apart-and-american-leaders-are-in-denial/

147 Rebecca Vilkomerson et al., *Solidarity Is the Political Version of Love: Lessons from Jewish anti-Zionist Organizing* (Haymarket Books, 2024), p. 264.

148 Shane Burley and Ben Lorber, *Safety through Solidarity: A Radical Guide to Fighting Antisemitism* (Melville House, 2024), p. 220.

149 Aaron Maté, 'Gabor Maté on the Misuse of Anti-Semitism and Why Fewer Jews Identify with Israel', *The Grayzone*, 6 November 2019, https://thegrayzone.com/2019/11/06/gabor-mate-on-the-misuse-of-anti-semitism-and-why-fewer-jews-identify-with-israel/

150 Jasmine Garsd, 'For Some Jewish Peace Activists, Demands for a Cease-Fire Come at a Personal Cost', *South Carolina Public Radio*, 28 October 2023, https://www.southcarolinapublicradio.org/2023-10-28/for-some-jewish-peace-activists-demands-for-a-cease-fire-come-at-a-personal-cost

151 Allan C. Brownfeld, 'For Judaism, it Is Increasingly Clear, Zionism Was a Dangerous Wrong Turn', *WRMEA*, 5 June 2023, https://www.wrmea.org/north-america/for-judaism-it-is-increasingly-clear-zionism-was-a-dangerous-wrong-turn.html

152 Anna Baltzer, 'Hamas Didn't Attack Israelis Because They Are Jewish', *Common Dreams*, 12 November 2023, https://www.commondreams.org/opinion/hamas-attacks-not-antisemitic

153 meital yaniv, *Bloodlines* (Communities of Memory, 2023), pp. 126-7.

154 Neve Gordon, 'Antisemitism and Zionism: The Internal Operations of the IHRA Definition', *Middle East Critique*, 33.3 (2024), pp. 345–60, https://10.1080/19436149.2024.2330821

155 Mark Braverman, email to author, 'NYT Letter Passover 2024', 20 December 2024.

156 Chris McGreal, 'How Pervasive Is Antisemitism on US Campuses? A Look at the Language of the Protests', *The Guardian*, 3 May 2024, section US news, https://www.theguardian.com/us-news/article/2024/may/03/college-gaza-protests-antisemitism

157 Donna Nevel, 'Stop the Killing in Gaza. Opposing Israel's Genocide Isn't Antisemitic.', *The Palm Beach Post*, 11 May 2024, https://

www.palmbeachpost.com/story/opinion/columns/2024/05/11/jewish-palestine-israel-gaza-antisemitism/73625944007/

158 Open Letter, 'Ten Holocaust Survivors Condemn Israel's Gaza Genocide', *Mondoweiss*, 22 June 2024, https://mondoweiss.net/2024/06/ten-holocaust-survivors-condemn-israels-gaza-genocide/

159 'Voices from the Streets of Chicago: DNC Protesters Call for Gaza Ceasefire & Economic Justice', *Democracy Now!*, https://www.democracynow.org/2024/8/19/dnc_protests

160 Abraham Joshua Heschel and Susannah Heschel, *Moral Grandeur and Spiritual Audacity: Essays* (Farrar Straus & Giroux, 1996), p. 225.

161 Rebecca Pierce [@aptly_engineerd], 'The 2 Main Constituencies Organizing for Gaza Right now Are Palestinians Whose Family Members Are under the Bombs, and Progressive American Jews, Many of Whom Lost Family in the Hamas Attack. This Is an Incredible Coalition that Should Give Everyone Courage. No Excuse, Speak up', *Twitter*, 18 October 2023, https://x.com/aptly_engineerd/status/1714727733706784926

162 Nisa Khan, '"Apocalyptic Horror Movie": What Bay Area Volunteers Witnessed in Gaza, the West Bank', *KQED*, 24 October 2024, https://www.kqed.org/news/12010352/apocalyptic-horror-movie-what-bay-area-volunteers-witnessed-gaza-west-bank

163 *Solidarity in Heartbreak with Rabbi Mordechai Liebling*, dir. by Pendle Hill, The Seed: Conversations for Radical Hope, 2024, https://www.buzzsprout.com/2032871/episodes/14792701-solidarity-in-heartbreak-with-rabbi-mordechai-liebling

164 Linda Holtzman, 'As a Rabbi, Taking Direct Action Against Genocide Is Part of My Sacred Practice', *Truthout*, 7 October 2024, https://truthout.org/articles/as-a-rabbi-taking-direct-action-against-genocide-is-part-of-my-sacred-practice/

165 Alissa Wise, 'I'm a Rabbi Who Hoped to Take Food into Gaza. Instead I Was Arrested.', *The Philadelphia Inquirer*, 9 May 2024, section Opinion, http://inquirer.com/opinion/commentary/israel-hamas-war-gaza-famine-rabbis-for-ceasefire-alissa-wise-20240509.html

166 'Naomi Klein: Jews Must Raise Their Voices for Palestine, Oppose the "False Idol of Zionism"', dir. by Amy Goodman, *Democracy Now!*, 24 April 2024, https://www.democracynow.org/2024/4/24/naomi_klein_seder

167 Sophie Hurwitz, 'How Anti-Zionist American Jews Are Organizing for a Ceasefire in Gaza', *Teen Vogue*, 8 December 2023, https://www.teenvogue.com/story/anti-zionist-american-jews-organizing-for-ceasefire-gaza

168 Ilana Levinson, 'Rabbi Miriam Grossman: "We Act and We Do not Wait for Hope"', https://www.unsettledpod.com/episodes/2024/2/13/rabbi-miriam-grossman-we-act-and-we-do-not-wait-for-hope

169 Viktor E. Frankl, *Man's Search for Meaning: An Introduction to Logotherapy*, 3rd edn (Touchstone, 1984), p. 154.

170 Brian Walt, 'As a Rabbi Raised in South Africa, I Can't Ignore Israel Is an Apartheid State', *Truthout*, 17 February 2021, https://truthout.org/articles/as-a-rabbi-raised-in-south-africa-i-cant-ignore-israel-is-an-apartheid-state/

171 Jesse Benjamin, 'Why I Protested the Jewish National Fund', *Mondoweiss*, 12 October 2010, https://mondoweiss.net/2010/10/why-i-protested-the-jewish-national-fund/

172 Sofia Orr, 'In War There Are no Winners. Refusal Statement.', *Instagram*, 2 March 2024, https://www.instagram.com/p/C4BdmAJNudI/

173 Mattan Hellman, 'The Problem Is Not a Specific Soldier, It Is the Entire Army | Refuser Solidarity Network', 5 May 2024, https://mailchi.mp/refuser/the-problem-is-not-a-specific-soldier-it-is-the-entire-army-refuser-solidarity-network?e=6843101bb9

174 Yuval Green, 'I Fought in Gaza, and I Am Part of the Growing Refuser Wave | Refuser Solidarity Network', 5 August 2024, https://mailchi.mp/refuser/i-fought-in-gaza-and-i-am-part-of-the-growing-refuser-wave-refuser-solidarity-network?e=6843101bb9

175 Zoe Guy, 'Joaquin Phoenix and More Support Jonathan Glazer's Oscars Speech in Open Letter', *Vulture*, 5 April 2024, https://www.vulture.com/article/oscars-2024-jonathan-glazer-speech-full-transcript.html

176 JTA and ToI Staff, 'Over 150 Jewish Creatives Sign Letter Supporting Jonathan Glazer's Oscars Speech', 6 April 2024, https://www.timesofisrael.com/over-150-jewish-creatives-sign-letter-supporting-jonathan-glazers-oscars-speech/

177 Lily Greenberg Call [@LGreenbergCall], Tweet, *Twitter*, 15 May 2024, https://x.com/LGreenbergCall/status/1790835052374360348

178 Avi Steinberg, 'Israeli Citizenship Has Always Been a Tool of Genocide—So I'm Renouncing Mine', *Truthout*, 26 December 2024, https://truthout.org/articles/israeli-citizenship-has-always-been-a-tool-of-genocide-so-i-renounced-mine/

179 Marc H. Ellis, *Toward a Jewish Theology of Liberation: The Challenge of the 21st Century*, 3rd expanded edn (Baylor university press, 2004), p. 224.

180 'An Open Letter from Jewish Students', *The Brown Daily Herald*, 7 November 2023, https://www.browndailyherald.com/article/2023/11/an-open-letter-from-jewish-students

181 Ian Berlin, 'Opinion: I'm a Jewish Student at Yale. Here's What Everyone Is Getting Wrong about the Protests', *CNN*, 27 April 2024, https://www.cnn.com/2024/04/27/opinions/yale-student-palestinian-protests-berlin/index.html

182 *Solidarity in Heartbreak with Rabbi Mordechai Liebling*, dir. by Pendle Hill, The Seed: Conversations for Radical Hope, 2024, https://www.buzzsprout.com/2032871/episodes/14792701-solidarity-in-heartbreak-with-rabbi-mordechai-liebling

183 'Israeli Holocaust Scholar Omer Bartov on Campus Protests, Weaponizing Antisemitism & Silencing Dissent', dir. by Amy Goodman, *Democracy Now!*, 30 April 2024, https://www.democracynow.org/2024/4/30/omer_bartov

184 'Ex-Brandeis President on Gaza Protests: Schools Must Protect Free Speech on Campus', dir. by Amy Goodman, *Democracy Now!*, 2 May 2024, https://www.democracynow.org/2024/5/2/campus_protests_frederick_lawrence

185 Ben Lorber, 'Toward a Sober Assessment of Campus Antisemitism', *Jewish Currents*, 28 November 2023, https://jewishcurrents.org/toward-a-sober-assessment-of-campus-antisemitism

186 Ryan Quinn, 'Tenured Jewish Professor Says She's Been Fired for Pro-Palestinian Speech', *Inside Higher Ed*, 27 September 2024, https://www.insidehighered.com/news/faculty-issues/academic-freedom/2024/09/27/tenured-jewish-prof-says-shes-fired-pro-palestine

187 JVP, 'An Open Call to Fellow Jewish Academics from Jewish Voice for Peace Academic Advisory Council', *JVP*, 13 May 2024, https://www.jewishvoiceforpeace.org/2024/05/13/

an-open-call-to-fellow-jewish-academics-from-jewish-voice-for-peace-academic-advisory-council/

188 Peter Beinart, 'The Campus Protests Make Me Uncomfortable. And They Fill Me with Hope.', *The Beinart Notebook*, 28 April 2024, https://peterbeinart.substack.com/p/the-campus-protests-arent-perfect?utm_medium=email&r=nvb5

189 Howard Zinn and Keeanga-Yamahtta Taylor, *You Can't Be Neutral on a Moving Train: A Personal History of Our Times*, reprint edn (Beacon Press, 2018).

190 Ilana Levinson, 'Rabbi Miriam Grossman: "We Act and We Do Not Wait for Hope"', https://www.unsettledpod.com/episodes/2024/2/13/rabbi-miriam-grossman-we-act-and-we-do-not-wait-for-hope

191 Meryl Crean, email to author, 'Shana Tova', 2 October 2024.

192 Rebecca Vilkomerson et al., *Solidarity Is the Political Version of Love: Lessons from Jewish Anti-Zionist Organizing* (Haymarket Books, 2024), p. 266.

193 Rebecca Alpert, '"Ceasefire Now!" Means Peace for All and Justice for Palestinians', *Truthout*, 28 December 2023, https://truthout.org/articles/ceasefire-now-means-peace-for-all-and-justice-for-palestinians/

194 Jamie Stern-Weiner, 'Gaza After the Deluge', *Jacobin*, 29 December 2023, https://jacobin.com/2023/12/gaza-war-israel-occupation-history-war-crimes-hamas-humanitarian-catastrophe

195 Shaul Magid, *The Necessity of Exile: Essays from a Distance* (Ayin Press, 2023), p. 300.

196 *Prophets Outcast: A Century of Dissident Jewish Writing about Zionism and Israel*, ed. by Adam Shatz (Nation Books, 2004), p. 330.

197 *Breaking News and Analysis on Day 299 of Gaza's Al-Aqsa Flood | The Electronic Intifada Podcast*, dir. by The Electronic Intifada, 2024, https://www.youtube.com/watch?v=ZkWFq_Wu2Us

198 Brant Rosen, 'We Charge Genocide: The Shofar Calls Us to Account on Rosh Hashanah', *Truthout*, 3 October 2024, https://truthout.org/articles/we-charge-genocide-the-shofar-calls-us-to-account-on-rosh-hashanah/

Organic olive trees with ripening olives on a sunny day. Photo by: Alina Bitta. iStock, https://www.istockphoto.com/photo/closeup-view-photography-of-organic-olive-trees-with-ripening-olives-at-sunny-blue-gm1550235693-526353429

About the Team

Alessandra Tosi was the managing editor for this book.

Hannah Mermelstein and Alessandra proof-read this manuscript.

Jeevanjot Kaur Nagpal designed the cover. The cover was produced in InDesign using the Fontin font.

Annie Hine typeset the book in InDesign and produced the paperback and hardback editions. The main text font is Tex Gyre Pagella and the heading font is Californian FB.

Jeremy Bowman produced the EPUB and PDF editions.

The conversion to the HTML edition was performed with epublius, an open-source software which is freely available on our GitHub page at https://github.com/OpenBookPublishers

Hannah Shakespeare was in charge of marketing.

This book was peer-reviewed by an anonymous referee. Experts in their field, these readers give their time freely to help ensure the academic rigour of our books. We are grateful for their generous and invaluable contributions.

This book need not end here…

Share

All our books — including the one you have just read — are free to access online so that students, researchers and members of the public who can't afford a printed edition will have access to the same ideas. This title will be accessed online by hundreds of readers each month across the globe: why not share the link so that someone you know is one of them?

This book and additional content is available at
https://doi.org/10.11647/OBP.0481

Donate

Open Book Publishers is an award-winning, scholar-led, not-for-profit press making knowledge freely available one book at a time. We don't charge authors to publish with us: instead, our work is supported by our library members and by donations from people who believe that research shouldn't be locked behind paywalls.

Join the effort to free knowledge by supporting us at
https://www.openbookpublishers.com/support-us

We invite you to connect with us on our socials!

BLUESKY	MASTODON	LINKEDIN
@openbookpublish.bsky.social	@OpenBookPublish @hcommons.social	open-book-publishers

Read more at the Open Book Publishers Blog

https://blogs.openbookpublishers.com

You may also be interested in:

For Palestine
Essays from the Tom Hurndall Memorial Lecture Group
Edited by Ian Parker
https://doi.org/10.11647/OBP.0345

Democracy and Power
The Delhi Lectures
Noam Chomsky; introduction by Jean Drèze
https://doi.org/10.11647/OBP.0050

Peace and Democratic Society
Edited by Amartya Sen
https://doi.org/10.11647/OBP.0014

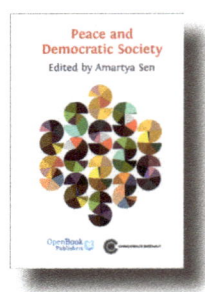

'Fragile States' in an Unequal World
The Role of the g7+ in International Diplomacy and Development Cooperation
Isabel Rocha de Siqueira
https://doi.org/10.11647/OBP.0311

www.ingramcontent.com/pod-product-compliance
Lightning Source LLC
Chambersburg PA
CBHW041314240426
43669CB00024B/2980